THE GRASS ROOTS PRESS:
America's Community Newspapers

THE GRASS ROOTS PRESS:
America's Community Newspapers

by

𝕵𝖔𝖍𝖓 𝕮𝖆𝖒𝖊𝖗𝖔𝖓 𝕾𝖎𝖒

The Iowa State University Press, Ames, Iowa

JOHN CAMERON SIM, a former weekly newspaper editor and publisher, is professor of journalism, University of Minnesota, where his field of special interest has been community journalism. Besides this book he has written articles for the professional journals of his field and he has continued his research in central printing plant operations for weekly newspapers and the development of the suburban press. His memberships include Phi Beta Kappa, Sigma Delta Chi, the American Association of University Professors, the American Civil Liberties Union; he is honorary member of the Minnesota Newspaper Association and has been director of the Minnesota High School Press Association.

© 1969 The Iowa State University Press
Ames, Iowa, U.S.A. All rights reserved

Composed and printed by
The Iowa State University Press

First edition, 1969

Standard Book Number: 8138-0335-7
Library of Congress Catalog Card Number: 69-17999

TO MARY LOU, ERIN, AND JOHNNY

PREFACE

As a former weekly newspaper editor and publisher, I have retained a natural interest in developments in the field. For some years now I have been actively seeking out expressions of views on its future. In my present capacities as a teacher and as placement chairman for a school of journalism, I have been made keenly aware of the concern of editors about the need for a continuing flow of professionally trained replacements in their field, and their concern for what will happen if the flow continues to diminish at its present rate. I have observed the widely shared fears that the community press in the small cities, towns, and villages is fading toward extinction in the not-too-distant future.

This, then, led me into studies of population movements, social and economic changes in the smaller community, studies of community leadership and power structures, as well as of technological changes and developments in the newspaper field. The time now seems appropriate for an examination of the functioning of the community newspaper and the many forms it has taken in the past and exists in now. My purpose is to offer some conclusions about the viability of this form of the mass media, its longer-range prospects, how swiftly it may change, and the forms any changes may take.

In gathering material for this volume I have been cordially received by scores of newspaper editors and publishers, and by a number of press association managers and officers, far too numerous to name, and I wish now to thank them. My discussions with rural sociologists and with researchers in suburban change and development have been most illuminating and helpful. I am responsible, rather than they, for any interpretations and conclusions drawn. Obviously, moreover, I am the one at fault for areas in this complex and changing field which may have been slighted or neglected here. No pretense is offered that this examination of the weekly newspaper field is definitive or complete; it is one observer's view of the outlook for the community press.

I have depended heavily on the trade press, as will become apparent from the text, for reports of current developments in the weekly newspaper field and for many of the exchanges of opinion among editors. I wish to record here my admiration for the dedicated efforts of editors of these periodicals in support of an improved and more vigorous community press. I am especially indebted to the splendid work of Rick Friedman in his regular column, "The Weekly Editor" in *Editor & Publisher*, and for his perceptive reports from conferences and conventions in which weekly newspaper editors and publishers participate.

Finally, I wish to thank Dr. Robert L. Jones, director of the School of Journalism and Mass Communication at the University of Minnesota, and other officers of the University, for making possible the single-quarter leave of absence from my University duties which provided the time necessary to complete the writing of the book.

JOHN CAMERON SIM

CONTENTS

INTRODUCTION

UNLESS they forget to check their datebooks, a group will gather at *Look* magazine's office building in Des Moines, Iowa, in 1987 to open a "time capsule." When the capsule was sealed in 1958, one item it contained was a description of the way advertising men believe life in 1987 will be. One such prediction was written by William H. Kearns, former president of Ted Bates and Co., one of the nation's top ad agencies, who wrote that by 1987 "daily newspapers will increase circulation in proportion to population, but few weeklies and semi-weeklies will survive as the smaller towns and communities expand their populations."

A third of the thirty-year period for which Kearns forecasted has now passed. How cloudy was his crystal ball? Was he right in predicting that the weekly newspaper is an institution which will virtually disappear within a comparatively few years? This book provides some clues for answering that question, with an examination of weekly newspapers and their role in the past and present, and a prognosis for the future.

This book will depart from the usual textbook treatment of editing and management problems in favor of evaluating the community press as a social instrument. This, to be sure, is not a pioneering effort, though almost all other studies of this nature have either been fragmentary or incidental to some other main topic.

xi

It seems that the weekly press has been and is yet so pervasive that it is taken for granted; no one beyond those most intimately affected pays much more than casual attention. It was the first type of newspaper we had; it continued even when other types began and flourished; it underwent no striking or abrupt changes in format or function; it maintained its usual vigor in the face of innovations of staggering social impact (radio and television); and it is likely to continue in much its same form in a forthcoming period of vigorous technological change.

This is not to say that the weekly press has existed and persisted in anonymity—witness the scores and hundreds of books by and about community newspaper editors, the countless texts that tell the student and practitioner how to perform every newspapering function. But when "the press" is studied, the weekly is nearly always lumped in with the daily. And though it is true the two are similar in basic operation and function, there are also a myriad of differences which this book will explore.

As Eric Sevareid remarked, "A lot of newspapers were founded by men with something particular to say, and who wished to say it." For a long time it became progressively harder to establish newspapers, yet no other method quite as satisfactory for propagating a point of view has yet been devised. One point made in the following chapters is that conditions are coming full cycle now and once again it is becoming feasible to establish some sort of newspaper with very little capital or technical skill or practical experience.

There are those who predict the decline of weekly newspapers on the basis of the large numbers of papers that have wasted away in the past half-century. It is believed by this author that this very fact tends to support the contention that the community newspaper (using the term in its broadest sense) will survive and flourish. Reasons will be examined and it will be shown that for progress to be made some of the traditional types must give way, just as the buggy gave way to the automobile.

We will not be so rash as to predict what the next half-century will bring in the area of physical format and methods of production and distribution, although some speculations will be offered in the final chapters. It will be predicted, though, that essential functions will remain much the same because human nature and human wants will remain the same. There is no doubt that the news consumer of the future *will be able* to get his news and opinion in exotic electronic forms, but it is doubtful that the demand for this will be widespread.

For some time now practitioners in the mass media have been concerned with "noise," the barrage of selling and informational messages of all kinds that assails the eye and ear every waking hour. We are all aware of the tendency (and need) to tune out the messages of lesser interest and impact, and that this tuning-out takes various forms. It is suggested in a later chapter that this developement may cause the mass media to lose some of their massive characteristics, even while expanding those which basically have to do with the production and distribution of messages. Thus, while it is likely we will have more "units" in the newspaper field, these separate units will take on more of the characteristics of the community paper than the metropolitan daily—reinforcing the slogan newspaper ad men like to use: "All business is local." As a result, however fantastic the world of the computer may become, a chief result may be conglomerates of units, not the growth of huge, monolithic structures. As evidence, witness the fact that a general national daily newspaper could be (in some respects is) available today, but there is no wild rush to buy it.

How will the new technology affect the "desire to be heard"? Evidence will be cited that more efficient technological methods will cause small newspapers, even one-man "underground" operations, to proliferate. Historical background will show that the recent wave of underground newspapers is but a manifestation of an old, and in the main honored, characteristic of the small weekly.

And how about the crusading editor? What part is he playing today and what will be his role in the future? It will be maintained in this book that the examples cited of crusading editors are not those of a vanishing breed, but of persistent types who will inevitably grow in number as population pressures increase. Idealism, too, will flourish, because otherwise world conditions threaten to become intolerable. With idealism will come greater emphasis on a truly professional dedication, of which the most significant mark will be the desire to serve the community.

TRADE PUBLICATIONS in the past couple of decades have been
assiduous in collecting from public leaders comments bearing
on chances of the weekly newspaper for survival. To a great
extent these reflect the stereotype that the community newspaper editor has the closest rapport with and truest understanding of "grass roots opinion": a view not really borne out by
scientific polling techniques or the results of national elections.
Pessimistic views are probably ignored because very little of
that nature shows up, as demonstrated by the following digest
of comments collected over a period of years from prominent
public officials and business leaders:

Small community dailies and weeklies are certain to grow and
have an increasing influence on state and local government, because of their closeness to the everyday affairs of the people. They
are not in competition with the metropolitan dailies, but rather
supplement them. As the large metropolitan dailies devote more
and more space to national and international affairs, the importance
of the community newspaper increases.—Abraham Ribicoff (when
governor of Connecticut).

We value the opinions of . . . community editors because we
know they are in continual close contact with their readers, who
are among the best informed people in the state.—Stuart Symington
(U.S. Senator, Missouri).

It is most essential for the small newspaper to continue to
flourish as a vital force in American life. As national and international problems grow in complexity, the common-sense expressions
of the weekly newspaper editor as told to his neighbors and fellow
townsmen must continue unhampered and unharmed. . . . The
weekly newspaper can and will grow with its community—America
needs it.—F. M. Flynn (former president and general manager of
the New York Daily News).

I believe the weekly papers are, far from declining, becoming
even more important in our lives. . . . The bigger a newspaper
grows, the harder it becomes to give the individual reader the
personal attention he obviously seeks and which the weekly paper
is so much better prepared to offer.—Leroy Collins (former governor
of Florida).

The weekly newspaper . . . constitutes one of the most permanent and beneficial institutions on the American scene . . . it
reflects, as the city newspaper never can, the whole aspect and total
life of the community and of the individuals dwelling therein. . . .
The value of the weekly newspaper in the social, economic and

political progress of the area it serves is incalculable.—*Harold Cooley* (U.S. Representative, North Carolina).

The importance of the country weekly in the life of our nation can hardly be over-estimated. . . . Close to the people, this last great stronghold of personal journalism in America is the pulse and voice of the community.—*Senator Lister Hill* (Alabama).

The outstanding government in Iowa, and the high standard of living enjoyed by its people, are in greatest measure attributable to the upbuilding influence of those who guide the destinies of our weekly press.—*Bourke B. Hickenlooper* (former U.S. Senator, Iowa).

The country newspaper is closest to the hands, hearts and lives of the people at the grassroots than any other publication. The country publisher and editor knows the needs, desires, and aspirations of his readers as no one else can.—*O. K. Armstrong* (U.S. Representative, Missouri).

The country editor is more than a journalist. Essentially he is an educator moving the hearts and minds of his readers. The influence he wields resembles that of a good teacher. Thus, like a good teacher, the country editor in the United States not only imparts facts, but consistently champions and exemplifies the moral and spiritual values that are the fountainhead of our national greatness.—*Roy E. Larsen* (president, *Time* magazine).

There is nothing that will ever replace the home-town daily or weekly in the minds and hearts of most Americans. . . . It would be a sorry day for America if we did not have our home-town newspapers to record their doings.—*Lee H. Bristol* (Bristol-Meyers Co.).

The country weekly has a sense of identification with its readers that is possessed by no other type of newspaper. At the same time I believe that the country weekly acts as a form of social cement in holding the community together . . . the country weekly newspapers . . . have helped to keep me in touch with the type of "grass roots" thinking which every public servant should bear in mind constantly. I believe that America would be the poorer should any catastrophe ever remove the country weekly from our life.—*Lyndon B. Johnson* (when he was U.S. Senator, Texas).

These glowing tributes should be laid beside the surveys which indicate that fewer than half of all the weeklies in the country regularly run any kind of editorial comment, either in the form of conventional editorials or as personal columns. Furthermore, it is clear that among those papers which do offer

measurable opinion content, a sizeable number just offer syndicated, clipped, or "planted" editorials which would offer a
poor, sometimes even misleading, evaluation of that "grass
roots" sentiment of which so many leaders spoke so glowingly.

It is still true, of course, that regular and close reading of
the *news* and *advertising* columns in a number of weeklies from
a selected area would afford a perceptive and analytical reader
a pretty fair understanding of trends and opinions in the area.
But he would have to start with a good knowledge and understanding of the people in the audiences of those newspapers.

WHILE it is true that the appearance and performance of many
weekly newspapers justify some skepticism about the urgency
of any need to keep them in existence—and at their worst they
can be very, very bad—at their best weeklies can be superb. As
a type of enterprise the weekly press has much the same
strengths—and the same weaknesses—as the ordinary man, if
such there be. These traits (the fact that it is generally a small
business is one) put the weekly newspaper as a social institution
much closer to that somewhat mythical figure "the common
man" than other types of the mass media.

THE GRASS ROOTS PRESS:
America's Community Newspapers

Chapter 1

UNITY IN THEIR DIVERSITY

THE COMMUNITY NEWSPAPER's greatest glory and strength is at the same time a reason for its weakness as a social force and for a seeming obscurity among the mass media of communication: it is so personal. The readers of a weekly tend to regard it with a proprietary interest ("our hometown paper") and they see its virtues or tolerate its defects just as they do for members of the immediate family. At the same time they are likely to have only the mildest interest in any other weekly newspaper, just as there tends to be a sharp drop in interest and concern for people outside the family circle. In short, the weekly newspaper has better acceptance as an individual than as a class.

It is quite understandable, then, that some prophets of the mass media will deprecate the vitality of the weekly and predict a relatively early demise for this kind of publication. Each observer is familiar with one community newspaper (his "own") or at best with a few, and may base his judgments on too limited a sample. He is not likely to add up the totals to find that even after a half century of decline community weeklies outnumber all the other units of the news-reporting mass media put together—all the daily newspapers, all the radio stations, the television stations, and the news magazines. This must be because weeklies are small units, and even collectively their financial statistics are not impressive in comparison to the other media. No one of them has the visibility of a New York

3

Times, a Los Angeles *Times,* a *Time* magazine, a clear channel radio station, or a metropolitan television station.

To a family, the hometown paper will have as much visibility as any one of the communication giants, yet evidently it is not easy for the family to comprehend thousands of similar, yet diverse, hometown newspaper situations. Considered as individual units, few if any weeklies have any national influence. It is their individuality, and their attention to a *local* scene, which gives them their greatest value and is the strongest attraction for both their owners and their readers.

The number of weeklies and the diversity of viewpoints they can represent may make them more a national asset than is currently realized if a recently advanced view of the First Amendment gains wide acceptance. Jerome A. Barron, an associate professor of law at George Washington University, proposes that the First Amendment be interpreted as not only protecting the press against government tyranny, but imposing upon the press an affirmative responsibility to publish minority views.[1] Since theoretically the Federal Communications Commission requires such an effort of the broadcast media through its "fairness doctrine," Barron's proposal would seem to be aimed at newspapers. The practical difficulty of imposing any such responsibility upon large metropolitan dailies appears to be immense, so one solution for society would be the active encouragement of more community weeklies representing varied points of view.

One of the great contributors to statistics that show the number of newspapers which have lived and died in our country has been the individual's desire to be heard on a broader scale than is usually possible in face-to-face oral communication or by letter writing. Studies made to determine why and how editors and publishers came into, or have remained in, the community newspaper business have turned up a preponderance of replies like these:

It (the newspaper) provides a vehicle for the printing of our ideas, and good ideas gleaned from others.

It offers the opportunity to serve the public and that is one of the greatest satisfactions of all—to serve your fellow man.

---

[1] Professor Barron prepared a "non-legal version" for the "Shop Talk at Thirty" column of *Editor & Publisher,* January 6, 1968, p. 52.

I am involved in a broad variety of activities in my local community with people I know.

By its nature, the newspaper business puts me "in the know" on most of the events in the community. Therefore I am constantly learning while informing.

I have access to every door, can talk to any person, can participate in almost any activity in the community or state. If I'm doing a reasonably good job, I have a place in the community that has some respect.

Because it is working with people, it is dramatic, it is challenging, it is adventurous; it forces me to work hard creating new ideas, taking new materials to manufacture a newspaper every week.

I feel like I'm my own boss.

Weekly newspapers from the very beginning have come in all shapes and sizes, produced under an almost incredibly wide variety of conditions by editors and publishers having an equally wide variety of qualifications (or lack of them). Some papers have been astoundingly hardy, existing under conditions about on a par with those in which the Indians of Tierra del Fuego live; others have been so frail that they expired in infancy even though attended by specialists. There are even hand-set weekly newspapers existing in this day of the machine. The picturesque conditions under which many newspapers have been kept alive have lent themselves well to the sort of fictional treatments and the first-person accounts to which many sober-sided, businesslike publishers vehemently object. A Wisconsin editor wrote:

The weekly newspaper people of America stand badly in need of a good press relations secretary, some smart guy in the know who can drastically change the public image of the weekly newspaper editor which has been so grossly distorted by books, movies and, more recently, television. Over the years I have read several books dealing with the small-town publishing business, all non-fiction of a single type; a courageous young couple from Park Avenue, fed up with city life, purchase a run-down little weekly newspaper back in the hustings. Then for 300 pages the author describes all manner of quaint happenings with a manner so patronizing it would gag an Italian headwaiter. . . . I once saw in a comic strip a word which describes this type of book to perfection. It was Ecccchhhh![2]

---

[2] "I'd Rather Be Right," column by Bob Wright, editor of the *Marquette County Tribune*, Montello, Wis., March 3, 1966.

The point of this and similar plaints is that the achievements of literally thousands of substantial, financially secure weekly newspapers, performing a vital community service in a responsible way, are obscured to the point where too large a portion of the public may believe the "quaint happenings" truly represent the community weekly.

What Is It?

What are we talking about when we discuss the weekly newspaper? Thomas F. Barnhart[3] distinguished among three types which he called:

(1) Small-town, in preference to the widely used terms "country weekly" and "rural weekly";
(2) Suburban;
(3) Community, by which he meant weekly, or less-than-daily, newspapers situated in and serving neighborhood areas of large cities.

(In the sense that many persons use "community" this is paradoxical, Barnhart points out.)

Concern over the vitality of the small town weekly is at least several decades old. Malcolm M. Willey, one of the first sociologists to study the weekly, said in 1926 that the function of the country weekly was narrowing and "recognizing this there are many who have argued that it cannot justify its existence at all. To them the country weekly newspaper is a survival that has long since outgrown its period of utility. They see it as an institution that has numbered days." His study, however, found "no conclusive proof" that the country newspaper was dying; all that could be said was that its function and scope were changing.[4]

In the years since Willey wrote, the function and scope have indeed changed. There are anachronistic specimens not markedly different from the little Connecticut weeklies he

---

[3] Before his death in 1955, Professor Thomas F. Barnhart of the University of Minnesota School of Journalism had won the appellation, "Mr. Weekly Newspaper," for his textbooks in the field. The classification of weeklies appears in *Weekly Newspaper Writing and Editing* (New York: Dryden Press, 1949).

[4] *The Country Newspaper* (Chapel Hill: The University of North Carolina Press, 1926).

studied, but they can be compared to the Model T Fords that occasionally chug along at rallies of antique automobiles. Conscious of an attitude that regarded the village paper with tolerant amusement, some editors shied away from the term "country weekly" and wanted to substitute other titles. A president of the Georgia Press Association urged his colleagues, "Let us take the term country weekly, let us take it and carefully and tenderly polish it up, label it with explanations and put it in the MUSEUM of antiquity and let it there forever remain. Let us abandon our pride in being publishers of *country weeklies,* for in reality they are no longer *country,* if successful, no matter the size."[5] This seems to imply that a yardstick of success could be applied, that the "successful" paper should be called something else. The Georgian's choice was "community weekly."

Yet, as Barnhart's classification indicates, that term had been assigned a special meaning by those who have studied 20th century weekly newspapers. Another sociologist whose work gained wide attention, Morris Janowitz, wrote:

The urban community press is defined as including any weekly (or more frequent) English language publication addressed to the residents of a specific locality or area of the metropolitan district. Four themes in general encompass the main elements of the image of the community press as held by its readers: (1) The community press is generally perceived as an auxiliary to the daily press—not as a competing news source. . . . (2) The community press is not generally perceived as a medium which is "commercialized." (3) The community press is not generally perceived as political or partisan but rather as an agent of community welfare and progress. (4) The community press is generally perceived as an extension of the reader's personal and social contacts because of its emphasis on news about voluntary associations and on local news of a social and personal nature.[6]

Some effort has been made to popularize the term "hometown papers," but small dailies quickly picked up the label, too, and the point was made that the industry might be confusing advertisers into believing that newspapers are divided into categories which include those of the hometown variety and

    [5] C. J. Broome, Jr., former president of the Georgia Press Association, speech reported in *The Iowa Publisher,* January, 1958.
    [6] "The Imagery of the Urban Community Press," *Public Opinion Quarterly,* Fall, 1951.

those that are not hometowners. If the term was to be just a distinction between metropolitan and nonmetropolitan newspapers, then it wouldn't be justified either, because the "mets" could rightfully claim their primary interest was in their "hometown"; we do not have general national, or even truly regional, newspapers.

Professor Wilbur Peterson of the University of Iowa, in writing about the role of the weekly, accepted the term "community newspaper" but specified that the category excluded "class weeklies, racial weeklies, agricultural weeklies, religious weeklies, and legal publication weeklies," and should include the approximately 420 daily newspapers published in places of less than 10,000 population, with less than 10,000 circulation, justifying their inclusion on the grounds that these smaller dailies "are performing essentially the same role that the weekly newspaper does, but with greater frequency."[7]

The confusion naturally extends to readers. Dorothy M. Johnson, then manager of the Montana Press Association, once tried asking a few people selected at random to explain the difference between newspapers and magazines, and found that the typical answer was that newspapers come out every day and magazines don't. Then, after reminding respondents that not all newspapers are published daily, she asked them to describe the major difference between a weekly and a daily, and got the answer: "Weeklies concentrate on social news."

And Sometimes It's Twins

Another aspect is that many newspapers which surely consider themselves in the category of weeklies do not in fact publish once a week, but twice or even three times. Then there is the phenomenon of the "twin weekly" which usually has developed from a merger—the publisher retains the names of both entities involved in the merger, publishes twice a week under these separate names but the papers are produced in the same plant, by the same staff, have the same ad and subscription rates, same type faces, and virtually identical circulations. To avoid too close an examination by the post office, the publisher

[7] "Role of the Community Press," *National Publisher*, May, 1962.

usually makes sure that the circulations do in fact differ to a minute degree.

Some effort has been made, too, to popularize the term "grass roots press," and it recurs frequently in the interviews solicited from political figures about the role and importance of the small town weekly. This term suffers from the same drawbacks of a lack of exclusivity and a vagueness of definition which affect the label "community."

Indeed, the ambiguity extends to "newspaper" as was borne home forcibly on the author recently when two FBI agents visited his office to solicit a definition of the term "newspaper." When this approach resulted in only a generality or two, they produced a sheet obviously used for the prediction of college football game results and which quite as obviously under appropriate conditions, could be used to provide support for the outcome of wagers. "Would you call this a newspaper?" they asked.

The immediate reaction was to say that of course this 8½ x 13 inch single sheet, ruled off into columns, printed with names of college teams paired for games on a specified date, spaces provided for predictions of score spreads, a column showing "point spreads," and very little else could not possibly be called a newspaper. Where was the news in text and pictures, the advertising, the cartoons, all the other outward aspects we have come to associate with the newspaper whether it be produced by letterpress, offset, duplicating machine, or even (as in the case of some early-day frontier papers) by handwriting? Then as we started to examine the various definitions of a newspaper—and a rather surprising number have accumulated over the years—it became evident that a skillful defender might be able to stretch each item of definition to cover this wagering sheet. Certainly it would not qualify under post office standards for admission to the second-class mail privilege, but there are many publications accepted as newspapers which fail on one or another of the post office points. Specialized information? The sheet provides it, of a sort. General information appealing to a variety of audiences? The appeal of football cuts across all classes and types of people.

Each item ticked off tended to support the agents' concern that a defense could be used that this little sheet, as it stood and without further evidence that it had actually been used in a wagering operation, could legally be circulated in interstate commerce under protection of "freedom of the press." At that stage the agents had seized only the copies of the sheet, and apparently had no testimony from bettors. The upshot was that the U.S. district attorney decided not to prosecute in that particular case—he felt that the defendants would be able to make their claim of protection under the First Amendment to the federal Constitution stand up.

Defining a Community

Similar difficulty may be encountered in pinning down a satisfactory definition of "community" as it might be applied to a segment of the press. Edward E. Lindeman, in his classic essay on the community[8] finds at least three relevant definitions of that term:

(1) The community in its "explicit elements" is any consciously organized aggregation of individuals residing in a specified area or locality, endowed with limited political autonomy, supporting such primary institutions as schools and churches. This is the traditional sociological concept of community and obviously applies to the village, town, or city.

(2) The community in its "implicit elements" is any process of social interaction which gives rise to more intensive or extensive attitudes and practices of interdependence, cooperation, collabora-tion, and unification. The stress is not on a geographic area or a group of people, but on a process that operates in an area or group; it is not a place but a process by and through which people are learning to relate to one another in such a way that capacity for cooperative and collaborative living is developing.

(3) The functional community, which would include those groups of people in any geographic area who share a common function or interest of sufficient importance in their lives to induce recognition among them of a common bond which draws them together in asso-ciation and organization, such as a group of welfare agencies com-bined into a Council of Social Agencies.

As indicated in the newspaper definitions given by Barn-hart and others, the kind of newspaper we are considering is usually classified as "small," which leads to attempts to define

------

[8] "Community," *Encyclopedia of the Social Sciences.*

what is meant by a small community. Wayland J. Hayes in *The Small Community Looks Ahead* defines it as "one which may be comprehended by a large proportion of its people through direct experience. Although the size and density of the population and the extent of the area are ultimately limiting and complicating factors in the definition of a small community, they may vary widely . . . there is no exact limit of numbers which makes such direct comprehension impossible."[9]

The difficulty of making generalizations about the community and therefore of the kind of newspaper which may be said to represent it is pinpointed by *Fortune* magazine: "Nor can the way of life be defined by the life of any one particular community—the late Sinclair Lewis to the contrary notwithstanding. For it is at the community level that America really begins to get diverse, because American life is not regional but local. The life of one town is influenced by a newspaper editor who wrote a history of his county and is a specialist on Indian warfare; the life of another by a doctor interested in psychology. . . . And yet, also, the way of life is *all* of these; for there is an extraordinary unity in all this diversity."[10]

The point that American life is not regional may be significant for those who ponder predictions that eventually the United States will have a system of regional dailies. To an extent we have representatives of this type of newspaper now, large dailies which cover whole states, or serve parts of several states. Improvements in equipment, communication, and transportation will certainly make the regional daily more and more feasible. The question remains whether in the next 50 or 100 years Americans will grow away from their present preoccupation with the local community. Developments to date cannot be encouraging to the advocate of regionalism.

To these problems of definition must be added a consideration of a distinctive type of community which has become a pervasive feature of the American scene, the suburb. One illuminating study, *Urban-Suburban Family Structure and Media Use* considered a number of definitions. These ranged from the loose and sweeping criteria used by Scott Greer: ". . .

---

[9] Hayes, in collaboration with Anthony Netboy, *The Small Community Looks Ahead* (New York: Harcourt, Brace & Co., 1947).

[10] The Editors of *Fortune*, with the Collaboration of Russell W. Davenport, *U.S.A.—The Permanent Revolution* (New York: Prentice-Hall, Inc., 1961). The inner urge motivating an editor may be epitomized in the book's quotation from Tocqueville: "If an American were condemned to confine his activities to his own affairs, he would feel robbed of half of his existence."

it can mean simply the outer edges, the residential spillover of the city, the little bedroom community, the home of the organization man, the upper-class municipality or the dead level of the American middle-class society," to the tight, undoubtedly too-restrictive definition attributed to Otis D. Duncan and Albert J. Reiss, Jr.: ". . . places of 2,500 or more inhabitants within the urbanized area but outside of the central cities."[11]

In any case, when we speak of a suburb, we know that we are dealing only with the definition of community which involves geographical area, though this does nothing to simplify the pattern of the many social, economic, ethnic, racial, religious, and other differences which mark such communities.

It is plain that the core of the difficulty in agreeing upon a term which specifically describes and delimits the role of the weekly (or less than daily) newspaper derives from the great diversity of types of operations which can lay some claim to recognition under almost any label used. This is not greatly different from diversity in other types of business, of course, but it is made more vivid by what is often called the "quasi-public role" of the newspaper at the same time that it is fully recognized as a privately owned and conducted business, and by the fact that the newspaper as either an institution or a business takes on a coloring from the personality of its owner and editors in a way not common to other enterprises, even among the mass media.

The daily newspaper, for instance, ordinarily requires substantial amounts of capital to found and maintain, and to that extent it is inescapably set apart as "big business" from a great part of its reading constituency. The weekly, on the other hand, is usually (but not always) a relatively small business. Most of its advertisers are small businessmen. The publisher and his staff have close contacts, in the same way his retail advertisers do, with the farmer, the workingman, the housewife.

The Weekly Flexes Its Muscles

But now there is a type of community newspaper that partakes of the advantages of both the big and the small, a

[11] F. Gerald Kline, *A Preliminary Report on Urban-Suburban Family Structure and Media Use* (Minneapolis: Communications Research Division, School of Journalism and Mass Communication, University of Minnesota, 1966).

"third force" we will discuss in detail later, one which operates in comparatively small units dealing closely and directly with the residents of a defined community, yet which is often indisputably a "big business."

An example may be cited which is certainly not typical but which is not unique either, and which may represent something of a pattern for this "third force" in the future. It is the Sun Newspapers of the St. Paul–Minneapolis metropolitan area. This group was formerly named the Twin Cities Suburban Newspapers, and as it was built up by John Tilton and associates each of the units retained its original name—*Review, Record, Reporter, Courier*, etc. After Tilton sold control in 1967 to Carroll E. Crawford, who merged his Lake Minnetonka area papers into the group, all twenty-six newspapers were given the name of *Sun (Fridley Sun, St. Louis Park Sun*, etc.). In this way the group has an essential unity, but the community name on each nameplate assures an individuality and a close community tie.

It was only in 1962 that the Twin Cities Suburban Newspapers, aching with growing pains, made a big investment in a building and a new press to convert to offset. In many ways at that time, Tilton was pioneering in the offset process, and scores of publishers, not only from all around the United States but including a few from abroad, visited his plant to study his methods. In just a couple of years the Goss Suburbanite press was found inadequate in capacity to handle the growth in circulation and in pages printed, and Tilton installed the first Goss Urbanite. By 1968 the new publisher, Carroll Crawford, found the plant and press capacity too limited and invested a million and a half dollars in a new plant in Bloomington, Minn., equipped with a seven-unit Goss Urbanite which has a capacity of fifty-six standard-size pages. Sophisticated computer equipment will speed both typesetting and business office operations. The firm has more than three hundred employees and is doing a volume of around five million dollars a year (partly in directory and other commercial printing) with the annual gross rising swiftly and steadily. The significant aspect in all this is that in just fourteen years the group exploded from a nucleus of three rather staid community weeklies on the outskirts of Minneapolis to the 1968 organization composed of twenty-six papers ringing almost the entire metropolitan area. This puts the operation in the upper classes as far as newspaper

operations are concerned, yet, as Crawford says, each of the
newspapers is directed to a defined and local audience—and he
intends to keep it that way. "This obviously is where our
strength is, and to be effective in the community the paper must
remain local."

The Sun Newspapers hold to the view that they complement, rather than compete with, metropolitan dailies, and that
their growth is as inevitable as the population shift to the
suburbs seems to be. Executive Editor Don Heinzman says,
"The suburbs are not remote from the problems normally attributed to the inner city; we have unemployment, blight,
growing pains, traffic snarls, and all the rest. And the suburbs
are not disconnected from the city in looking for a solution to
these problems. They've become everyone's concern. To relate these questions of today to the suburban resident—a suburban newspaper does it best."[12]

Everyone's concern. The residents of the metropolitan
core city, of the suburb, of the rural small town and village.
Yet concern is keenly felt by Everyman only when a problem
"hits him where he lives." Nothing can better describe the mission of the community newspaper than to say it exists to report
on and to comment about the affairs and problems of the community—and that hits Everyman. It's the reason why we can
expect a basic form of the weekly newspaper to exist even
though in its externals it may change drastically. The size of
the investment the Sun Newspapers and other groups like it
around the country are wagering on the continuance of a demand for separate, recognizable community newspapers is solid
evidence that shrewd, progressive businessmen believe the
sophisticated hardware in mass communications predicted for
the future will only strengthen the community weekly.

Revitalizing Nonsuburban Areas

If it is agreed that the diversity of the weekly press, the
opportunity it offers for many voices to be heard, is beneficial
to our society, what chance is there for capital investment

[12] Comments by Crawford and Heinzman from "Sun Newspapers—Suburban
Success Story," *Format* (monthly magazine of the Advertising Club of Minnesota,
Minneapolis), May, 1968.

similar to that we have noted in suburban situations? On the record up to the present time, very little chance. Therein would seem to lie an opportunity for service for one of the many foundations that have sprung up in recent years. One of the severest handicaps for a small weekly as an independent enterprise is the lack of capital and of access to low-cost, long-term loans needed for efficient operation. Newspapers and broadcasting stations are not eligible for Small Business Administration loans (most journalists would agree that it is proper they are not). It would not take large resources, as modern foundations go, to set up a loan program for young publishers who need money to modernize a plant or to join with other publishers in an area to construct a centralized printing plant, or to found an entirely new newspaper. Individual loans could be small, really just adjuncts to commercial lines of credit already available. The important point is that these loans in a range of perhaps $10,000 to $50,000 be for long terms and at modest interest rates.

This could help bring into the field the young, vigorous, educated talent it needs, and to retain those who might otherwise become discouraged and move into other occupations. The foundation naturally would set up a screening program to assure that loans go to operations that have the potential for repayment of the loans. The applicant would have to have an equity in the enterprise substantial enough to assure that he won't just casually abandon the enterprise under adverse conditions. Here there would be an opportunity to bring more representatives of minority groups into the field of mass communications, and they would be coming in at a level where they could make the greatest contribution toward the solution of minority problems, in close contact with the people. The kind of views or philosophy espoused by an applicant for loan assistance must NOT be a consideration; the whole purpose of such a program would be to assure a diversity of opinion and opportunity for it to be voiced. A disinterested foundation would be in far better position to provide such assistance than any corporation, and certainly it would be immensely preferable to any kind of formal government program. It is likely that the foundation would find it could make its aid felt most effectively through assistance in construction of centralized printing plants for smaller communities in rural areas.

If it is argued that there is no reason why a foundation should make loans to community newspapers in preference to other types of privately owned business, say popcorn stands, the peculiar quasi-public role of the newspaper may be cited. The earlier mention of a theory of a public access to the press, to complement the public's right to know, assumes this quasi-public status. It underscores the point, too, that the foundation's loans all ought to be relatively small because the aim would be to open up opportunity for more individual voices to be heard, both of editors and of the public. Thus a foundation with assets in the range of fifteen to twenty million dollars could aid hundreds, eventually thousands, of small papers, and as repayments and interest payments came in, the fund would be self-perpetuating.

Role in a Technological Society

If it is hard now to define a newspaper, and if the concept of the *community* newspaper is a little slippery, the vistas opened for us by the technologists promise to make the problem of definitions immeasurably harder. News will continue to be evaluated as news, but it will reach us faster, in a different form, through a different method of distribution, presumably for somewhat different methods of consumption.

Most of the exotic systems and equipment—the photoelectric readers, the communication satellites, the computers, voice recognition systems, the cathode ray and laser beam, the image-transfer devices—which are to contribute ultimately to what has been called a home communications center for the average household all are intended to increase the volume and flow of news and background information. Fewer promises are made about improved quality of that flow.

Yet just about the most common complaint of men and women in the professions and business is the difficulty—nay, the impossibility—of keeping abreast of the volume of "must reading" in their fields. The best that the elaborate information retrieval systems now being developed can promise is that the nuggets of useful and desirable information need not be irretrievably buried and that they can be located more quickly and easily, not that the time required to absorb them will be lessened or that the volume of them will be decreased. Added to this is the nagging feeling that as a responsible citizen the business or professional man should keep well informed about the increasingly complex problems of the day—foreign affairs, civil rights, pollution, poverty, inflation, and many others. A technology which vastly increases the flow of information into the home will not change the basic human being and his preferences to any much greater extent than the current ready availability at the corner newsstand of hundreds of paperback books, scores of magazines, and dozens of local and out-of-town newspapers do now. Certainly these may widen some horizons and redirect some interests, and so will the beautiful technology of the future. We can be sure that newer methods of education and improved understanding of the processes of cognition will make the person of the twenty-first century able to comprehend more in less time, and to retain it longer. Still, a strong argument can be maintained for the view that this flood of information will tend to bend the individual back upon himself, to make him more selective in his reading and viewing, to concentrate his interests upon the problems that touch him most directly; in short, to make him a better customer for the *community newspaper,* in whatever form it may take in the future.

Isn't that basically what is happening now in the flurry of interest we find in what is loosely called "the underground press?" It is not at all underground in any of the senses in which we have previously used that term. It resembles nothing more than it does the special forms of nineteenth-century weeklies we will describe more in detail later—the political party papers, the publications representing forms of agrarian unrest, the foreign language journals for enclaves of immigrants, the little papers serving the uprooted in mining camps, in railway labor gangs, at emigrant reception stations.

The most marked difference today, of course, is that reports of *news* are so pervasive that the alienated and uprooted almost literally cannot avoid them. They have to make a deliberate, conscious effort not to see commercial daily newspapers or news magazines, not to listen to newscasts, or to see television news. So the impelling force isn't that hunger for news which encouraged the proliferation of so many small newspapers in the last century. A writer who examined the so-called underground newspapers says " . . . but they ask not to be judged on content. They do not think of themselves as newspapers, offer no news."[13] They are journals of opinion, of comment on topics and in areas which the established media do not cover or into which they will not venture. These papers represent an intense desire on the part of the editors, publishers, and contributors to be heard, to have a place to express an opinion publicly.

The recording and transmission devices of the new technology all are designed to increase vastly the *inflow* of information into the home and office. The effect can only be to multiply many times the problems of selection the individual faces even today. Even now, of course, a person theoretically could read, listen to or look at sources of information and news twenty-four hours a day. Wherein will the home information center change that? The very person who could most closely approach this hypothetical news saturation point would be the least likely to remain a passive receptacle into which the endless quantities of information are poured. He wants to react, to make *his* opinion known or felt. And this is the reason for the underground press today, as it was for the political party newspapers or the frontier papers of an earlier day.

Journalists agree that the means (the printing press, microphone, television tube, or whatever) of conveying and distributing the news are secondary, even rather incidental, to the basic processes of gathering, sifting, and reporting the news. About equally important may be evaluating and commenting upon that news. All this must be done with a specific audience in mind. The material intended for the broadest, most general audience undergoes an inherent and inevitable loss of more specialized fragments within a general audience. So the satellites, the laser beams, the computer-operated devices can bring more news from farther points in less time, and their very success will tend to satiate the audience. That age-old question "What's in it for ME?" will have to be answered at the local level, and therein lies the continuing opportunity for the community newspaper.

Just as the underground editor is more interested in

---

[13] Ethel G. Romm, "Protest Tabloids Turn On To Color Printing," *Editor & Publisher,* November 11, 1967. Mrs. Romm quotes one editor, "It is easy enough to start a paper. It is very hard to keep it up."

opinion and comment than news, however, so must the community newspaper of the future provide a more effective vehicle of opinion. It must serve the individual frustrated by that vast inflow of news because he lacks a feeling that he can react effectively to it. Thus it won't necessarily be the editor's opinion, as it was in the nineteenth-century papers, but it should be more the opinion of that citizen in his home communication center with its facsimile printer and its three-dimension TV screen and its visual telephone and all the information cascading in upon him. The free forms which the underground papers take seem to give readers much more opportunity and freedom to express views which are unorthodox either in kind or in manner of expression. Therein may lie a lesson for the community newspaper of the future.

In still another respect present-day newspapers of protest may offer a refutation to the pessimistic advertising agency executives who foresee a decline of the weekly press because they do not believe it can remain an efficient, economical medium in the face of more sophisticated types of competition. These papers are the antithesis of the commercial, free-circulation publications which exist almost solely on advertising revenue; these newcomers maintain themselves almost entirely on circulation income. To be sure, most of them do carry advertising (often of a type commercial publications refuse to carry) but to a significant extent the papers make a satisfactory profit just on single-copy sales. As the explosive improvement in printing processes continues, it will assure that these copies can be produced at lower cost, thus increasing the margin of profit for both publishers and distributors. Then, paradoxically enough, the evidence of keen reader interest provided by these single-copy sales will bring advertisers back clamoring for space. Eventually, no doubt, many far-out protest publications may find themselves becoming regular members of the Establishment. And though they now have as their "declared enemies, the established press and in turn established society," they have adopted some of the visible signs of the established press such as "at least two underground news agencies, roughly comparable to the Associated Press and the United Press International of the regular world."[14]

[14] Thomas Pepper, "Growing Rich on the Hippie," *The Nation*, April 29, 1968.

Pessimistic predictions about the community weekly take into consideration chiefly the number of newspapers which have died in the past or are now being merged or discontinued. The underground newspapers provide a perfect illustration of the life processes in the journalistic jungle—they spring into life amid lush undergrowth, bloom for a few issues, then wither away as the moving spirits of the enterprise move away, lose interest, or just grow older, wiser, and sadder. That's the way it was, too, in the early vigorous days of our nation; that's the way journals of opinion have almost always fared. When a Harry Golden decides he is no longer able to carry on a *Carolina Israelite* he cannot or does not pass the torch to a successor.

So here is support for the contention that the news consumer of the future will continue to regard himself as first of all a member of a community (or a couple of different types of communities) and will want a *selection* of news and information that bears directly on his community concerns. As life becomes steadily more complicated his withdrawal into a comprehensible, defendable, reachable community is all the more certain.

A Practical Prognosis

Individuality is the strength and the weakness, the hope and the despair, of the community weekly field. However the social and economic patterns develop in the United States in the next several decades; whatever the impact of an amazing new technology; it is clear that hundreds of now existing weeklies will not long survive because their fields are inadequate or because their editors and publishers are inadequate or too resistant to change; in short, because they do not deserve to survive. Loans of the sort suggested here should not go to such applicants to help them eke out a few more years of inadequacy.

On the other hand, the greater number of today's weeklies will live on in essentially their present form for decades to come because they do have good fields, able editors, and concerned readers. One of the most encouraging aspects is the growing, though belated, realization among leaders in the field,

both rural and suburban, that they must make a more vigorous and sustained effort—through higher pay, better working conditions, earlier responsibility and opportunity to innovate—to recruit and retain young staff members on both editorial and business sides. Any strengthening of the financial condition of small newspapers which would lead toward these goals could be a significant public service for the kind of foundation activity suggested here.

A most significant aspect of the younger generation is an avowed desire to do something worthwhile for society; to serve. The evolution of the weekly newspaper traced in the following chapters shows that a similar desire motivated a very large number of young and vigorous editors from the Colonial days to the opening of the last western frontier. Today as then young journalists share a feeling of professional dedication best summed up in a somewhat paraphrased sentiment attributed to the late C. P. Scott when he was editor of England's great *Manchester Guardian:*

Upon this earth there can be no much greater responsibility than that involved in the control of a newspaper. All a man's days and all his powers, all the conscience that is in him, and all the application he can give are surely not too much fittingly to discharge so great a task.[15]

---

[15] As quoted by T. S. Mathews, *The Sugar Pill* (London: Victor Gollancz Ltd., 1957).

Chapter 2

FROM THESE BEGINNINGS

To give the news: Atlas, Repository, Messenger, Courier, Item, Herald, Press, Record, Town Talk;
   To offer opinion, guidance: Oracle, Advocate, Crucible, Monitor, Sentinel, Opinion, Exponent, Criterion, Mirror, Agitator, Hatchet;
   To promote trade and commerce: Advertiser, Bulletin, Clipper, Patent Trader, Pointer, Clarion, Bugle, Booster, Miner, Nugget . . . even Laramie Boomerang or Tombstone Epitaph;
   To represent a party: American, Union, Confederate, Unterrified Democrat, Republican, Citizen, Constitution, Nonpartisan . . . or an Eccentric, Philistine, Tiller & Toiler, Reformer, Other Side;
   To shed light: Sun, Moon, Star, Gem, Mercury, Reflector, Headlight, Searchlight;
   To communicate: Telegraph, Telegram, Telephone, Radiator, Camera, Locomotive;
   To reflect a locale: Avalanche, Glacier, Rustler, Scout, Frontier, Comanche Chief, Lyre, Palladium, Pantagraph, Nonpareil . . . the "great proud glittering names" that show the great range and diversity, the many roles of a weekly newspaper.

THE WIDESPREAD ACCEPTANCE of the weekly newspaper as an integral force in American life has its roots in the earliest days of newspapering in this country. For the earliest newspapers, of course, both in this country and in Great Britain, were weeklies. Not until 1783 did the first daily newspaper appear in the United States, although there were a number of papers of greater publication frequency than weekly. A reason for the avid interest in the community newspaper is cited by Edwin Emery:

Indeed, the press was more and more counted upon to supply the information, inspiration, agitation, and education of a society often unable to keep up with its need for schools. . . . In many communities, newspapers were the only literature available for the bulk of the citizenry. They served as the main educational device until other cultural institutions could take up the slack caused by rapid migrations.[1]

The tacit acceptance by editors of this responsibility for education of a sort shaped for a long time the form and content of weekly newspapers, and they changed more slowly than would have been justified by the rapid rise and spread of schools at all levels. The *Maryland Gazette* in 1742 said its purpose was to give a weekly account of "remarkable occurrences, foreign and domestic," but because transportation and communications were slow and unreliable,

. . . in the dearth of news, which, in this remote part of the world, may sometimes reasonably be expected, we shall study to supply that defect by presenting our readers with the best materials we can possibly collect, having always, in this respect, a due regard to whatever may conduce to the promotion of virtue and learning, the suppression of vice and immorality, and the instruction as well as the entertainment of our readers.[2]

The details of the dependence the Founding Fathers placed on weekly journals to introduce their views to the public are too well known to need repeating here. All through the early years of the nation, the weekly newspapers were the artillery with which major political parties supported their attacks or defended their positions. Modern readers frequently protest that political reporters go too far in quoting intemperate partisan remarks or charges, or that columnists are excessively frank about the shortcomings of officeholders. It would be salutary, before major political campaigns, to reprint more widely many of the comments and articles about the sainted figures of our early history, written by their contemporaries. To

---

[1] *The Press and America: An Interpretive History of Journalism* (2nd ed.; New York: Prentice-Hall, 1961).

[2] Paul Winchester and Frank D. Webb (eds.), *Newspapers and Newspaper Men of Maryland, Past and Present* (Baltimore: Frank L. Sibley & Co., 1905).

be sure, these are now offered occasionally as literary curiosities; they deserve a wider dissemination.

Surface behavior, at least, has changed, and we are more than vaguely uneasy now when we read vitriolic attacks, even on our bitter opponents. Yet at the same time there is a marked tendency to deplore what is called the blandness, the lack of force and individuality, in today's weekly newspaper. We say there is too much of "on the other hand," or "but, neverthe-less . . ." or "we realize others may disagree with us." Most of us insist that vigorous debate is desirable, and we urge more of it—but where is it to take place; how may the citizens engage in it? Radio and television provide a forum akin to the speaking platform of earlier days but in a hall infinitely extended. Their limitations, however, are obvious and promise to become more constricted rather than less. Our early politicians were not satisfied with the speech and the debate, though these were basic; they turned invariably to the written word, usually disseminated first in the weekly newspapers, then often reprinted the material in pamphlet form.

Now, in this writer's opinion, our large population inevitably speeds a trend toward factionalism, and the weekly press may once again come to perform a function similar to its role in the early days of the Republic—the factions will turn to their own weekly papers to carry on their debates, spread their doctrines, rally support. The large daily newspapers, the magazines, radio, and television all appear unsuited or inadequate for the role. Indeed, not a few present-day weekly newspapers, largely suburban, admirably serve as forums for debate in their own communities on local policies, problems, and personalities. There are even a few cases where opposition newspapers are painfully supported by minority factions, in the very image of the great days of the political party press. This chapter will review some of the difficulties and hardships faced by early editors, leading to the suggestion that economic and social difficulties will not be serious obstacles to the founding of new papers in the future.

To Inform and Agitate

As the new nation settled its Great West, weekly newspapers continued to serve these same ends of "information, inspiration, agitation and education," described by Emery. Another historian of American journalism, Frank Luther Mott, remarked that "Wherever a town sprang up, there a printer with a rude press and a 'shirt-tail full of type' was sure to appear as by magic . . . these pioneers were politically minded and they wanted newspapers to promote the spread of their favorite partisan doctrines. Hence it was that villages of only a few hundred would often have two papers of differing political faiths."[3] A third historian, James Melvin Lee, also noted this effect of news hunger: "The frontier printer occasionally started his newspaper before the arrival of other settlers. With intuitive foresight he seemed to know probable locations of settlements along rivers and at the junctions of smaller streams."[4]

Testimony comes from many sources about the eagerness of early settlers, whether in railroad boom towns or mining camps, trading posts or religious colonies to have their own newspapers. Robert F. Karolevitz has compiled many instances of the willingness of frontiersmen to pay high prices for copies of newspapers in his fascinating pictorial history *Newspapering in the Old West*. Much muted by the vast changes in our society, that desire to identify with a hometown newspaper is still the basic source of strength for the weekly and a pretty good guarantee that the institution will persist in a recognizable form for a long time to come.

That controversial student of the frontier, Frederick Jackson Turner, was not speaking directly about pioneer newspaper owners and editors, but his description of frontier traits certainly reflects the qualities which impelled them to produce their little sheets under conditions often incredibly difficult:

From the conditions of frontier life came intellectual traits of profound importance. . . . That coarseness and strength combined with acuteness and inquisitiveness; that practical, inventive turn of mind, quick to find expedients; that masterful grasp of material things, lacking in the artistic but powerful to effect great ends; that restless, nervous energy; that dominant individualism, working for good and for evil, and withal that buoyancy and exuberance which comes with freedom.[5]

We shall see these traits exemplified innumerable times as we examine some of the conditions under which the weekly

---

[3] *American Journalism* (New York: Macmillan Co., 1941).
[4] *History of American Journalism* (Boston: Houghton Mifflin Co., 1923).
[5] R. A. Billington (ed.), *Frontier and Section, Selected Essays* (Spectrum Book [New York: Prentice-Hall, 1961]).

press rose in numbers and influence during the youthful days of the Republic. Perhaps a cycle is to be found in a predicted return, to be noted in a later chapter, to conditions under which it will be possible to found little papers for "inspiration and agitation" with comparatively limited capital, and to keep them going on modest levels of income. The traits which came to the surface in frontier life have not been eliminated; they have been covered and softened, dispersed among a multiplied population, but in certain individuals and under certain conditions they can reappear.

A reason that the "hand press and shirt-tail full of type" became a cliché is the same one that creates most clichés—it was basically true. William Dean Howells, reminiscing about his youth in a small print shop, recalls about his father, "He had no money, but in those days it was an easy matter to get an interest in a country paper on credit. . . . An office which gave a fair enough living, as it was then, could be bought for twelve or fifteen hundred dollars."[6] That, of course, was in Ohio, an area scarcely considered, in that time, as any part of the "frontier." An Arkansas newspaperman, writing about the early days of the press in his state, said:

This number of papers is accounted for by the fact that it is an alluring business, and none is so easy to get into. Anybody can start a newspaper. Material could be bought on credit. One man relates that he had only $22 when he bought a half-interest in a country newspaper. Another says that he bought a newspaper for $400, $25 cash and the balance on payments. . . . Many editors can be traced from town to town. . . . There have been more than five thousand editors, publishers, and owners of newspapers in Arkansas in the last hundred years.[7]

Even though equipment was often cheap, and could be obtained on easy terms, it was rarely plentiful. There are authenticated instances of the practical inventive men of whom Turner wrote who constructed their own presses, on occasion entirely of wood, and used them successfully over quite a period of years. A tobacco can could become a printer's "stick" and a plank or a tombstone could serve as his imposing stone.

---

[6] "The Country Printer" (an essay reprinted for private distribution by the Plimpton Press, Norwood, Mass., 1896).
[7] Fred W. Allsopp, *History of the Arkansas Press for a Hundred Years or More* (Little Rock: Parke-Harper Publishing Co., 1922).

Some made their own inking rollers, occasionally of a mixture of glue and molasses, and Karolevitz recounts that one of the industrial hazards of the day was that Indians would steal these rollers and consume them like candy. The one item the early-day printer could not conveniently make or improvise was paper, and numerous are the tales of the lengths publishers were forced to go to maintain some continuity of publication. They printed issues on wrapping paper, wallpaper, blank sides of already printed sheets, even muslin or other cloth at times when transportation breakdowns, blizzards, floods, or other causes delayed or prevented the arrival of newsprint. Although credit was said to be easy, publishers did often run out of it, and the newsprint stayed in the express office because of a lack of cash to pay the freight charges. One historian quotes an editor on another excuse for a reduced edition of his paper:

APOLOGETIC—In consequence of our marriage we are compelled this week to appear on a half-sheet.

The writer then goes on to describe some of the difficulties with paper supplies. The qualities of initiative, persistence, endurance, and dedication shown ought to be edifying for a present-day generation struggling with problems of the weekly newspaper. He explained:

The half-sheet business was the *dernier resort* [sic] of every country editor who couldn't raise a sufficient number of quires for his next issue. As illustrating the chronic besetment of many of the earlier country editors, it may be stated as a fact that one editor of the period was known to have borrowed most of the stock from brother publishers on which his paper was printed during most of its precarious existence. The man traveled far and near—as distant as 30 miles or more—for a bundle of paper. And, generally, he got it. . . . Expedients to save time were necessary. . . . The borrower, belated, hastening home with his paper, would think "tomorrow is publication day and this paper must first be dampened." Coming to the first creek he would souse the bundle in it and let it stay ten minutes. By the time he reached the printing office his paper would be ready to "turn" and put under the weight. . . . In cold weather, in such quarters, wetted paper would freeze. The inevitable two days of press work in each week were fraught with difficulties that modern printers know little about.[8]

---

[8] H. L. Williamson, *History of the Illinois Press Association* (Springfield: Hartman-Jefferson Printing Co., 1934).

If it took comparatively little cash to start or buy a newspaper in the nineteenth century, those days of low wages, long
hours, and limited circulations also made the income requirements low. A publisher respected for his business acumen,
addressing his brethren at a convention in 1891 on "How Much
Ought It to Cost Per Year to Produce an Average Newspaper
of 1,000 Circulation?" arrived at a total expense figure of
$2,430 for the year. He considered that the labor of three per-
sons would be necessary and that the newspaper would be following the custom of the time in using readyprint. The ready-
prints could be had for 14 cents a quire, and the cost of paper
for a year, with express charges added, would come to about
$360.[9] He broke down the items of expense thus:

Wages (three employees)	$1,650
Newsprint	360
Rent	150
Ink and rollers	12
Power and other utilities	50
Postage, 2nd class and other	18
Fuel and oil	40
Taxes and insurance	35
Incidentals	15
Wear and tear [depreciation?]	50
TOTAL	$2,430

No doubt this budget would make the newspaper compare favorably with almost all other small business enterprises
of the community. Rates for circulation and advertising were
similarly low, and depression periods often made collections
difficult. Some of the tiredest humor about small newspapers
is drawn from editors' own writings about their poverty, or the
appeals they made for payment or barter items for subscriptions. Many, perhaps most, editors were poor managers of
credit and indifferent collectors of past-due accounts. But even
those who made a vigorous effort had reason to be discouraged;
one publisher of a small upstate New York weekly wrote that
"On one occasion, the result of my day's trip was the collection
of one dollar and a bushel of corn." The same man further
recalled that

. . . of some ten of my acquaintances, engaged in the business, but
two were earning enough to supply their daily necessities. The

---
[9] *Ibid.*

credit system was the ruination of nearly every paper. But few calculated to pay the subscription ($2.00) until the expiration of the year, and in order to worry it out of most of them at the end of the first six months, one must resort to the most humiliating expedient of portraying in the strongest, plainest language, the wants of family, and enter into minutest details.[10]

Naturally there were wild discrepancies in advertising rates, publishers usually just setting rates they thought they could get. As early as the Civil War period, however, there were some concerted efforts to achieve a standardization, and one Midwest committee submitted a schedule for consideration of fellow publishers, urging a system based on "One square, one week in papers of less than 500 circulation, $1 first insertion and 50 cents each additional insertion for the first four weeks. Papers of at least 500 circulation and less than 1,000, $1.50 for first insertion and 75 cents for each additional insertion for first four weeks. Papers having 1,000 circulation in no instance to charge less than these rates, but as much more as they think just."[11] A schedule was also listed for periods such as three, six, and 12 months and for five, ten, and twenty squares a year; for double-column advertisements and for cuts in advertisements, 25 per cent extra. (A square was defined as 250 ems, equivalent to eight lines of nonpareil, or ten lines of minion.)

The Urge To Convince

Why, in the face of such difficulties and with the promise of such limited rewards, were there so many newspapers? Why did publishers, having failed one place, go to another town to start a new newspaper, often under greater hardships than before? Whatever the reasons one might advance for this persistence, the same reasons can be cited today for the surprising number of papers in villages of less than 500 population, villages which have been declining over several decades and show little evidence of halting the decline, villages which simply do not have the retail business to provide adequate support for a newspaper. The reasons will be basically the same for the urge which results in the founding of new weeklies, often in the

---

[10] William H. Winans, *Live and Lively Reminiscences and Experiences in the Life of an Editor* (Newark, N.J. [no publisher given], 1875).
[11] Williamson, *History of Illinois Press.*

most unlikely places, and the urge which leads men and women successful in other media enterprises to buy and operate weekly newspapers.

An editor might say that his purpose in entering the profession was a "desire to serve" or, because of his political convictions, it was an urge to convince. The instances where just such impulses could have been the only possible reasons were far too numerous to permit any cynical interpretation. It was said of James King of William, fighting California editor who was slain in the early days of San Francisco, that "he started the Bulletin, convinced that such money as he might invest in the enterprise would be lost."[12] An editor wrote in 1837: "In conducting the Gazette no calculations of gain or loss are made by the proprietors or the editor. Our efforts are to make a useful paper and at the same time give it a tone above truckling in religion, morals, or politics."[13]

To be sure, various interpretations of the "power of the press" popularly believed to be inherent in almost any medium of mass communication undoubtedly lure many. In some cases this view of the power is laudatory:

We who are now living [1886], some of us, have seen them [newspapers] change from mere vehicles of intelligence to engines of immense power, closely connected with the peace and prosperity of the people and the nation . . . well conducted newspapers have a tendency to disseminate useful information upon all important subjects of every name and nature; to keep the public mind awake and active; to confirm and extend the love of freedom; to correct the mistakes of the ignorant and the impositions of the crafty; to tear off the mask from corruptions attempted by designing men; and finally, to promote union of spirit and of action among the most distant members of an extended community. Newspapers, to do all that is expected of them, must be conducted by men of talent, learning, and virtue, in order that they may continue to be public blessings. We may well rejoice in the constant increase and cheapness of these trusty teachers.[14]

On the other hand there were jaundiced views of the havoc caused by the unqualified:

---

[12] John P. Young, *Journalism in California* (San Francisco Chronicle: Publishing Co., 1915).

[13] Osman Castle Hooper, *History of Ohio Journalism*, 1793–1933 (Columbus: The Spahr & Glenn Co., 1933).

[14] John W. Moore, *Moore's Historical, Biographical, and Miscellaneous Gatherings Relative to Printers, Printing, Publishing and Editing* (Concord, N.H.: Republican Press Assn., 1886).

If a man wants to play the serpent of paradise generally, just let him dive into journalism, without experience or discretion. He will stir up strife between neighbors, ruin some person's character, get some good man killed, have the churches at loggerheads, split up the schools, cause some innocent person to go to the penitentiary, another to commit suicide, and demoralize the community generally.[15]

A sainted figure in the lore of small town journalism, William Allen White, had a similarly dyspeptic view of weekly newspapers in the nineteenth century. He wrote in his autobiography:

And now, because I have spent a lifetime as a country editor, it may be well to consider the country newspaper business in that day and time. In the mid-eighties of the nineteenth century, practically all American cities were country towns. In those distant days American towns were driven by factions—political factions based more or less upon commercial rivalries in the town. The banks quarreled bitterly and trivially, but ruthlessly. They generally financed, and virtually owned, the newspapers. The newspapers were beggarly at the best, and mendacious at the worst. A newspaper was an organ sometimes political, but at bottom and secretly, an organ of some financial group in the community which aimed at control of public utilities or public patronage of some sort or other. Occasionally an editor in a country town, who had a large job printing establishment, was independent. But his advertisers and subscribers rarely made him independent. He was too often, for all his pomp and bluster, the creature of his banker. . . . But too frequently the editor was a pasteboard hero, who, when the times changed and factional fighting ceased in America, caved in and went to the scrap heap—a disheveled, vain, discredited old pretender.[16]

Another of the giants of American journalism took a more dispassionate view of the duties, objectives, and opportunities of the small town editor and publisher. Adolph S. Ochs, who gained enduring fame as the publisher who molded the New York *Times* in its present-day form, came out to speak at the seventh annual convention of the National Editorial Association at St. Paul, while he was still editor and publisher of the Chattanooga (Tenn.) *Times.* He suggested that the requirements imposed on a small town editor and publisher (usually "united in one person") are greater than those in a large city;

<hr />

[15] J. M. Raines, editor of Fordyce (Ark.) *Enterprise,* quoted in Allsopp, *History of the Arkansas Press.*
[16] *The Autobiography of William Allen White* (New York: Macmillan Co., 1946).

that an all-around man is needed—practical printer, businessman, and of "gentlemanly habits." He advised that an editor
should be free of financial entanglements and under no personal obligations "to anyone who may seek to sway the paper
from pursuing a fearless, honest course in the discussion of all
public questions or in the treatment of men, measures, or incidents." Before an audience which no doubt included many
who were highly skilled in devising and applying scurrilous
names and epithets to fellow editors, Ochs maintained that an
editor "while aggressive and outspoken, [should be] always
courteous and respectful to those with whom he differs: mind-
ful ever of the fact that all people are not of the same opinion.
. . . He should bear in mind that fortunately the 'slinging of
mud' at newspaper men is one of the incidents of the profession
arising often from ignorance and blind prejudice, but most frequently from envy and jealousy." He urged his listeners to remember that it was not necessary to be a duelist or pugilist
"but it is necessary that he be made of such stuff that he fears
no one who prides himself on these barbarous characteristics."[17]

Hazards of the Calling

R. H. Henry, reminiscing about 50 years of journalism as
editor of the Jackson (Miss.) *Clarion-Ledger,* made reference at
one place or another in his book to eight killings of or by editors, and told of another five editors who had been severely
wounded at some stage of their careers.[18] Hamilton Cochran, in
his book, *Noted American Duels and Hostile Encounters,* devoted a fat chapter to duels involving editors. Many of the
pictures in the Karolevitz book show rifles, shotguns, and pis-
tols prominently displayed beside type cases or the editors'
desks.

Both the instability of a large segment of the early weekly
press and the exchanges of personal insults which led to duels
or other "hostile encounters" could be traced directly to the
prevailing view of the role of the community newspaper. Their

[17] Ochs' speech at NEA's 1891 Convention. *The National Editorial Association of the United States* (Chicago: B. B. Herbert) Vol. I, Proceedings of the first
ten years.
[18] *Editors I Have Known* (New Orleans: Upton Printing Co., 1922).

names contained the word "news" but the papers didn't do much to justify the appellation. It comes as a minor shock to many of today's newspaper readers to learn that local news or personal items began appearing with some regularity in newspapers only three-quarters of a century ago and later. Since the communities were small it was assumed that readers knew already what was going on in the home town; "news" was regarded as something from outside the community. Hence the practice inaugurated by the very first colonial newspapers of clipping or reprinting news and comment from exchanges continued down to the end of the nineteenth century (and, to some extent, continues today). Readers didn't really expect to find local news in their papers; some might even have resented it. "They're no good," a grizzled old Westerner said, "The newspaper asks us for the news, prints it, and then asks us to buy it!" The value that many eastern big city editors, led by the first James Gordon Bennett, perceived in certain types of local news did not become apparent to the editors in the hinterlands until much later. Successful young newspaper publishers like William Allen White did not share the preference for opinion over news. "We stressed local news," he recalled in his autobiography about his early days, "and printed a number of items that ordinarily would not have been printed in a strictly conventional newspaper. We were chatty, colloquial, incisive, impertinent, ribald and enterprising in our treatment of local events. Looking back over it now, I can see that much of it was based on a smart-aleck attitude, but the people liked it. . . . I set no great store by the editorial page. I believed that local news, if honestly and energetically presented, would do more for subscriptions and the Gazette's standing in the community than its editorial page. Indeed, I believed then and believe now that a newspaper that prints the news—all of it—that is fit to print, can take any editorial position it desires without loss of patronage or profit."

This is a credo endorsed by present-day editors, and doubtless this belief in the primacy of news has done much to lessen the vigor of editorial comment in modern weeklies and to decrease the number of papers which regularly carry an editorial page or column. Most observers will agree that the emphasis on news is highly desirable, but many will insist that the historic mission of the newspaper (any size) is (1) to offer news of a range and variety suitable to its audience; (2) to provide information of the marketplace through advertising; and (3) to give leadership through well-balanced opinion, interpretation, and evaluation.

A fourth ingredient often is added—entertainment. This is not to be interpreted in the sense of comic strips, humor columns, crossword puzzles, and other syndicated features, but news written so interestingly it can be said to entertain. It must be admitted that few community weeklies now can be said to perform this fourth function adequately. Frank Lindsay, when setting down principles devised from his long association with management of the successful Lindsay-Schaub group of newspapers in Illinois, had this in mind when he urged his co-workers,

Every column of news which we print should be carefully selected as being of interest to certain groups of our readers. There is a limit as to how many columns of reading matter we can print and keep the paper interesting to our readers. The ideal local newspaper is one so printed that a reader can relax in his own home and read quietly the accurate and interestingly written news about his neighbor and city for several hours without irritations.[19]

The ideal may seem less and less attainable as surveys show a steady reduction in time devoted to newspaper reading, but really all the surveys prove is that other media are more successful in entertaining, and newspapers therefore face a constant challenge to be more interesting without lessening accuracy, responsibility, and fairness.

Francis Williams, writing about the English press in *The Dangerous Estate* commented on a supreme example of one of the most profound of all journalistic truths—that "whatsoever would influence the public must first learn to entertain it." It must be agreed that many British newspapers have built huge circulations through skillful application of the principle. Arthur Christiansen, the great English editor who was perhaps the outstanding practitioner of popular journalism, readily offered his formula for success: "All my journalistic thinking is based on making the news so inviting to people that they read involuntarily news which normally would not interest them."[20]

[19] Arthur Lane, Jr. (ed.), *Observations From 46 Years of Newspaper Management* (Decatur, Ill.: Lindsay-Schaub Newspapers, Inc., 1960).
[20] *Headlines All My Life* (New York: Harper & Bros., 1961).

The fourth function, if thought of in that sense, must be the community weekly's weapon against competition offered by those media supremely competent in the entertainment field—radio and television. Something so basic as the news hunger will not change appreciably. The newspaper starts with this fundamental asset; its basic commodity is news, in both editorial and advertising columns. Success in the media will go, as it does to the restaurateur, to the competitor who can serve up the basic dishes in the most attractive fashion.

To the extent that the community press can attract and retain the talent able to write and edit most interestingly, to package and merchandise the product in an appealing way, the weekly can be assured not only of long survival, but could expand beyond anything now contemplated. It is in a strong position to offer what amounts to enticing bonuses for that talent, bonuses in the form of greater flexibility and opportunity for individuality, personal expression, closer contact with readers, and satisfaction in community service—if only publishers realize the inherent advantages of their medium and use them to best effect.

The view that the small newspaper is a helpless chip floating wherever the currents of the vast stream of our modern culture take it, and that it is doomed to a backwater eddy, is unduly constrictive. The weekly has numerous present-day models of what it can and should become, and these show that the community weekly has great power to shape and control its own destiny.

Chapter 3

HEYDAY OF THE AMERICAN WEEKLY

Editors are usually abstemious, but the Detroit *Press* speaks of an interior journalist who came to that city on business, and in some inexplicable fashion was induced to leave the straight and narrow path and take on more liquor than he could conveniently carry . . . he was robbed of his all, and was found in an alley the next morning by a policeman who advised him "You'd better go 'round to your friends and raise something."

"Friends be hanged," replied the editor. "It's only sixty miles, good going, and three days before my paper comes out, and it's not the first time I've been without a cent in my pocket."[1]

IF THIS ATTITUDE was then common among editors, it probably accounted for a proliferation of weekly newspapers under conditions which today would be regarded as unbearable. We have seen the testimony supporting the view that during most of the nineteenth century it took a small investment and little cash to start a weekly newspaper in small or new communities. In the expansive spirit of that day, the desire to "be my own boss" often struck printers soon after they had learned the trade. Because of the westward tide of migration, a spot to locate a new paper in was easy to find; much of the time the original settlers and businessmen of a town site were ready to offer enticing inducements to a printer looking for a place to settle.

There were frequent land booms, followed by just as fre-

---

[1] William H. Winans, *Live and Lively Reminiscences and Experiences in the Life of an Editor* (Newark, N.J. [no publisher given] 1875).

quent busts. Speculators bustled about trying to interest new businesses in the town sites. One printer, shown a plat of a new business district in such a boom town, asked what buildings now occupied the area. "Buildings?" responded the agent. "Why, my dear sir, this property is too valuable to be built on!"[2]

Pulling Back To Regroup

There are those who believe that American society has already changed so drastically from the early days that the need for the type of communication and information represented by the weekly newspaper is disappearing, and that a new technology will offer replacements for it in ways which are yet largely unspecified. In this chapter we will take a closer look at the weekly press of the last century and discover the reasons for its extraordinary vitality.

Will something as pervasive, so much a part of the traditional American scene as the weekly newspaper, die out? There has been a steady decline in numbers despite the nation's soaring population. Figures taken from directories for that time indicate that a high point of 17,005 weeklies and semi- or tri-weeklies was reached in the United States in 1915; the figure of publications accepted as "true newspapers" is less than half that today. The theory might be advanced, though, that newspapers are subject to the same laws of natural selection and evolution as the plant and animal world. Evidently Mother Nature or her typographical equivalent has allowed, in the usual lavish fashion allowed for oysters or rabbits or dandelion seeds, many more newspapers to germinate than the environment could sustain. The story is the same with settlements; thousands are not even "ghost towns" today—the only trace of many once-promising villages is to be found on old maps. Yet these towns often supported not one but several newspapers. The competition among settlements for the glory of a newspaper to spread the community's fame has been described rather typically:

Atop a wagon with his two small sons and his antiquated printing press, Andrew Logan, a Pennsylvania printer, jolted into the frontier village of Davenport [Iowa] on July 7, 1838, and promptly

---

[2] Beman Brockway, *Fifty Years in Journalism* (Watertown, N.Y.: Daily Times Printing & Publishing House, 1891).

found himself in the midst of a brisk controversy. Eleven villages in Iowa, projected and real, burst into full cry, clamoring for his newspaper, desirous of its prestige and promise of future growth it would bring them. Loudest of all were the cries of Davenport and Rockingham. Each would be the county seat, and each was lavish with its inducements to the printer with the wagon-borne shop that would help them to their goal. Each offered Logan his pick of the choicest lots . . . but Davenport . . . added ingenuity to real estate and dangled 500 guaranteed subscriptions before the printer's nose. The number was greater than the population to be served. . . .[3]

Historian David M. Potter explains that "For a people of whom 90 per cent followed agricultural pursuits, abundance meant the opportunity to settle the new lands. The government responded by a series of land laws, beginning with the Ordinance of 1785 and extending far past the Homestead Act of 1862, which made land progressively easier to attain, until at last they could acquire title to 160 acres absolutely free . . . quick settlement was stimulated even by legislation which encouraged squatters to occupy the land even before it had been opened to public entry. Relatively early, however, it became clear that access to soil did not mean access to wealth unless it was accompanied by access to market."[4] Thus the railroad building boom began and spread, but after the roads were built the population was usually too sparse to make the traffic profitable, and the railroads vigorously promoted European immigration.

Reference was made in the previous chapter to the ease with which printing establishments could be packed up and moved to new locations. It need not be regarded as too surprising, therefore, that Professor William Howard Taft of the University of Missouri, in the most exhaustive study ever made of newspaper mortality in a single state,[5] found names of more than 5,000 newspapers which had been published at some time or other in Missouri, and then he was not certain that he had discovered them all. He found that the number of papers in

---

[3] *The Lee Papers: A Saga of Midwestern Journalism* (Prepared by "colleagues of E. P. Adler on his 75th birthday, September 30, 1947" [Kewanee, Ill.: Star-Courier Press, 1947]). It may be a tribute to the power of the press to note that today Rockingham does not even exist, while Davenport is the state's third largest city.

[4] *People of Plenty* (Chicago: The University of Chicago Press, 1954).

[5] *Missouri Newspapers* (Columbia: University of Missouri Press, 1964).

Missouri reached its peak about the turn of the century when nearly 900 were listed in directories of that day. In 1956 the Bibliographical Society of America published a listing which said that Kansas led in the number of recorded newspaper names with 4,368, followed by New York with 3,309 and Pennsylvania third with 2,519.[6] Professor Taft's experience indicates that these listings must be far from complete.

In Party Service

Community pride was not the single, or perhaps even the main, reason for the multiplication of little weeklies and the presence of competing newspapers in villages economically unable to support one properly. Milton W. Hamilton, writing about the New York rural press, observed that "Politics may not have created the country printer, but he found his greatest activity in party service."[7] Few printers could be party leaders but they were always involved in party councils, often as secretaries or recorders of conventions or nominating sessions, and one historian has called them the antennae by which party leaders sensed the cross-currents of political life. If political sentiment in a village was fairly evenly divided (and it commonly was) the party not represented by a newspaper could rarely rest until it did have its own party organ.

This inevitably led to a type of bitterly personal journalism which is now just a historical curiosity—evolution has led from the era of the fang and the claw to a period now deplored as too bland and characterless. There must be a desirable middle ground between the view which held that an editor who never earns a flogging must be timid and irresolute in the management of his paper, and that which desired an absence of any comment or opinion at all. Five editors of the Vicksburg (Miss.) *Sentinel* were killed in street fights in ten years, leading an editor in another section to comment that "shooting editors seems to be the favorite amusement of the Mississippians." Collecting choice examples of invective from the columns of

---

[6] Reference from Leroy Brewington, "Kansas Has Had Most Newspapers," *The Kansas Publisher*, November, 1956.

[7] *The Country Printer, New York State, 1785–1830* (New York: Columbia University Press, 1936).

early-day weeklies is a happy pastime for many writers in the
field of newspaper history, and the following are offered as just
a few of the many fusillades exchanged at point-blank range:

Why, you lying varmit! you miserable toad-eater! you half-witted
blackguard! you abortion! you starveling, that came into the world
half-made up, to snarl and bite, to bark and growl, to howl—frighten
kittens and scare chickens from the hen-roost! You knew when you
first made the assertion that it was a lie . . . every inch a lie.[8]

Thirty years later the level of debate in the community had
risen a few points, taken a more urbane tone:

Our self-righteous down street contemporary, who, in the excess
of his egotism and piety, imagines it is his province not only to
regulate the great affairs of State, the minute affairs of his church,
and the gestures of public lecturers, but also the business of his
neighbors, reads the Press of this and other cities occasional lectures
on the subject of advertising, etc. Now we neither take all the medicine we advertise, read all the books, nor buy all the "gift jewelry"
or other wares, nor do we recommend to our readers to do so. Nor
do we think them so thick-headed as to take medicine they don't
need simply because we advertise it, or to expect to get rich by
investing $1 in some "gift-enterprise" because an advertisement
makes glowing promises. The Courier may have such an ignorant
and gullible set of readers—it would be natural if it should have—
and if so the editor does well to be cautious in the mental diet it
doles out to them either in his reading or advertising columns.[9]

In a way it is disappointing that the editor who composed
the following did not permit himself to be "betrayed into any
epithets" because it would have been interesting to see what he
could do if he really let himself go:

. . . If you place this circumstance with the fact that he is one of
the school of shriekers, after the order of those females who have
reversed the order of Providence by wearing breeches and ranting
at public lectures, the inference is clear that his visit to the South
was designed to alienate the blacks from their masters, and pre-
cipitate a horrible servile insurrection, which, in its abhorrent
course, would murder the grayhaired and helpless, and dash out
the brains of unoffending babies. What a monster of depravity

[8] Ann Arbor (Mich.) *Argus*, October 5, 1838; from Louis A. Doll, *A History of the Newspapers of Ann Arbor, 1829–1920* (Detroit: Wayne State University Press, 1959).
[9] Michigan *Argus*, January 10, 1966; from Doll, *Newspapers of Ann Arbor*.

this man must be! It is now known with certainty that this new editor, the malformed specimen of perfidy and brutality, this jaundiced miscreant with the heels of a black-a-moor, was guilty, while among our Southern neighbors, of the enormity of teaching the alphabet to a couple of small niggers, in direct violation of the law, in plain derogation of the rights of the master, and in direct antagonism to the requirements of a broad philanthropy and a comprehensive Christianity! It was our purpose, when we began this article, to preserve a calm and dignified composure, keeping aloof from those ebullitions of passion in which so many partisan sheets indulge. Although the provocation was coarse and abusive, we are glad we have not been betrayed into any epithets of a gross and scurrilous character. . . .[10]

The frenzy and froth of the Citizen quill-pusher is agonizing. He will have to be committed to the asylum for the feeble-minded before the campaign is over. He can't distinguish between personal abuse and legitimate argument. He never relished brain food, but his diet is evidently stale buttermilk, spoiled pickles, etc. Say, Nick, wash the dirt out of your ears just once, scrub your filthy teeth, and change the socks you have worn all summer, and you will look and smell better. Then you can turn your attention to filling the empty cavity in your cranium. The *Phonograph* deprecates the personalities; however, if the upstart does not desist from his sewer effusions, we will turn aside from our usual course to kick the mangy cur. . . . I wish here to brand the utterance a lie, unmitigated, malicious, damnable; prompted only by a desire to make capital out of a base misrepresentation, and that it is a sample of what has appeared in the *X-Ray* ever since it began its vile existence. . . . Last week's Ackley *Phonograph* was so slimy that it stuck in the mail and did not arrive here until Tuesday of this week.[11]

A Mean Blackguard—Captain *Consequence,* or in other words, *Charley Holt,* has been pleased, if he ever was pleased, to *daub* in his paper the following ridiculous paragraph against the editor of the *Honest American:* "A Dishonest American—The foolish rascal in Herkimer, who to the disgrace of the name of editor is the lickspittle of the *Public Advertiser,* cannot expect further newspaper notice, but will be silenced without disturbing our readers with so pitiful a subject." Capt. Charley talks of "silencing us," but the captain is informed that not he nor all the *men* he could raise while a captain in Hudson will be able to silence us. Capt. Charley says we cannot expect any further "newspaper notice." God grant that we may not receive any further notice from so mean a scoundrel. This "pitiful subject" wishes not to "disturb" his readers. It

---

[10] From an editorial directed at J. M. Dixon, quoted in his *The Valley and the Shadow; Comprising the Experiences of a Blind Ex-Editor* (New York: Russell Bros., Publishers, 1868).

[11] Ira A. Nichols, *Forty Years of Rural Journalism in Iowa* (Fort Dodge: Messenger Press, 1938).

is well known that as far as Capt. Charley's influence extends, he has done more to disturb the republican party than any other editor in the state. An eternal goodbye to you, Capt. Charley, unless you plan to take further notice of us than that of "newspaper."[12]

Mark Twain's classic satire on personal journalism, "Journalism in Tennessee," really could not exaggerate the bitterness that political and economic competition engendered. Whenever third parties entered the scene (Greenbackers, Free Soilers, Populists) the exchanges might grow even more frantic, and when wartime or religious tensions were added, words sometimes incited action. History is dotted with disgraceful episodes in which mobs destroyed Abolitionist, Mormon, or other minority newspapers. Even the courtesy due a lady might be forgotten under such stress. Arthur J. Larsen, who edited a collection of letters by Jane Grey Swisshelm, a pioneer Minnesota editor of the *Saturday Visiter (sic)*, writes: "On the night of March 24 (1858) three men . . . broke into the office of the Visiter. They destroyed the press, scattered some of the type in the street, and threw the rest into the Mississippi River. . . . Public resentment was aroused . . . and a number of the more stable businessmen of the town called a mass meeting . . . voted to procure a new press, new type, and sufficient capital for Mrs. Swisshelm to carry on the publication of the Visiter. . . ."[13]

Era of Readyprint

Problems of founding and financing political newspapers, which were often intended to last just for the duration of a campaign, were considerably simplified by the rise of the ready-print system, a service by which two, four, or other multiples of pages of material without much timeliness were printed in a central plant and the sheets of imprinted newsprint, with some space left blank, were shipped to country publishers who then printed the remaining pages from type set in their own shops. This enabled the weekly editor to produce a paper with more pages and a more varied, far-ranging content. Within three years after the A. N. Kellogg Company, the pioneer firm in the

---

[12] Hamilton, *The Country Printer* (from an item published in 1810).
[13] *Crusader and Feminist—Letters of Jane Grey Swisshelm* (St. Paul: Minnesota Historical Society, 1934.

field, had established its first branch house in 1873, there were at least fifty readyprint houses around the country. Thomas D. Clark, in his study of the Southern country editor, writes:

Working furiously, these houses sought business all over the country, and their Southern branches helped establish many new papers. . . . It was rather easy for a prospective editor to secure a sufficient supply of type, an antiquated press, and a bundle of readyprint pages and launch a weekly. The newspaper unions [readyprint houses] would supply the materials and equipment on reasonable credit terms. . . . The syndicates likewise stimulated the publication of spasmodic special-interest journals which lived through political and reform campaigns and then disappeared into well-merited oblivion. After 1875 there was a second syndicated service called "boiler plate" which saved setting type in the offices of country newspapers.[14]

The boiler plate came in one-column width, although cartoons or other illustrations might be wider, and in various lengths suitable to fill holes which might be left by an insufficiency of type set in the home plant. By 1880 the A. N. Kellogg Company alone numbered more than three thousand weekly newspapers among its patrons, indicating that virtually all country papers used readyprint, boiler plate, or both.

These services eased the production problems not only of political papers but another common type which had as its principal motivation turning a quick and relatively easy profit on the "proving up" notices required for homesteads. In areas where the free farmlands were filling up rapidly, this type of public notice could be decidedly lucrative, particularly if the publisher didn't invest much time or effort in publication—and readyprint was ideally suited to relieve him of a good share of the burden.

Public notice has a long, and to publishers honored, history in the American weekly press. One of the first of a long line of European critical observers of American press practices noted this. He was Professor Bernard Fay of the University of Clermont-Ferrand, who wrote after a trip to the United States in the 1790's:

We have to add that in the Eighteenth Century most of the editors of the newspapers were poor devils, badly paid, if paid at all, by their subscribers, of whom they complained often. This precarious

---

[14] *The Southern Country Editor* (New York: Bobbs-Merrill Co., 1948).

position made them all wish to become printers for the state; so they did not like to antagonize the established authorities and tried on the contrary to placate them. Such was the liberty, absolute in principle, and limited in fact, which was enjoyed by the American press. . . . It appears from these examples that by 1790 Americans had acquired the habit of announcing everything in the newspapers and of searching them for information of all kinds.[15]

One of the happiest aspects about homestead notices for lazy publishers was that the law required the notice to run for a number of weeks consecutively, presumably for the benefit of readers "searching for information of all kinds." Thus once a printer-publisher had a number of the notices set into type, he might have only a column or so of other space to fill during the week and could devote himself to commercial printing, or to the comforts of the saloon across the street. And though most publishers were content with this kind of easy-going operation, there were those, as always, who had visions of larger things. Daniel Whetstone, a pioneer Montana publisher, tells about one of these cases in his autobiography:

A fellow who had served a spell as receiver of the U.S. Land Office at Bowman, N.D., bought himself a "parent" plant and twelve "packhorse" plants—ones that can be moved from place to place on a horse's back, an exaggeration, of course. Well, he put the "parent" plant at Thunder Butte and twelve "packhorse" plants at crossroads post offices and back-country blacksmith shops. He must have known the attitude of the registrar at the Bowman land office. The proofs for all the packhorses were set in the parent shop. The one-sheet papers supposedly printed in the satellite places were also printed in Thunder Butte.[16]

The reason for the satellite papers was that the proof notices went to the newspaper published nearest to the quarter section of land involved. If the homesteader did not comply with the conditions involving a certain period of residence on, and cultivation of, the land, his claim was subject to contest, and Whetstone notes that "contest notices were longer and more revenue-producing than the proof notices. . . . The Registrar of the land office and U.S. commissioner were objects of

[15] *Notes on the American Press at the End of the Eighteenth Century* (New York: The Grolier Club, 1927).
[16] *Frontier Editor* (New York: Hastings House Publishers, 1956).

adulation and often beneficiaries of emoluments from the eager editors."

Another victim of abuses which grew up around the ready-print system was the infant institution of national advertising. The readyprint houses rather quickly convinced some businesses, especially dispensers of the patent medicines and cure-all nostrums which thrived with virtually no control in those days, that the community newspapers offered a convenient and effective medium to advertise the products over broad areas—*if* the ads were placed in a kind of single-order, single-payment system through the readyprint houses. Then, as now, national advertisers found that dealing with individual newspapers, with all their variations in rates, printing dates, equipment, column widths, and efficiency in handling orders could be just a staggering problem. The houses, in turn, offered the publishers the readyprint service at much cheaper prices because an important part of the costs was defrayed by the advertising. At the end of the 1880's typical rates ranged from nine cents a quire for a small sheet such as a five-column folio (the standard-size sheet folded once) to twenty-six cents a quire for eight-column quarto (the full-size sheet folded twice to make eight pages). Thus a publisher with a paper of about one thousand circulation could obtain his newsprint, with much of the composition and press-work already finished, for a little more than ten dollars per issue. The interest of the readyprint houses in offering these attractive prices should also be obvious—the larger the total circulation they could offer (number of newspapers times the circulation of each) the higher the rate they could charge the advertiser. As a result some houses were accused of inflating their circulation figures by exaggerating the number of newspapers they served. But couldn't advertisers scotch this deception by demanding tearsheets? They could, and did, and received the tearsheets—but still were sometimes deceived. A speaker at the 1893 convention of the Minnesota Editorial Association explained one way:

I have seen published in a town less than eight miles from here [St. Paul] a paper that had not a line of type changed for month after month with nothing set up in it except a single line of type—patent inside and patent outside. I do not know that it had a single subscriber. I never could find anyone who subscribed for it, and still the publication continued right along. . . . Now whether or not these patent houses are paid by their list of papers, for instance, for 200 or 300 papers to swell their list, I do not know.[17]

One of the firms, the Western Newspaper Union, seeking to establish better standards and more ethical practices, began buying up or merging with many of its competitors, and by 1910 had almost a complete monopoly of the printed services. At its peak it was serving more than seven thousand newspapers, in the mid-1920's this number had fallen to half, and in the spring of 1952, when the WNU discontinued its readyprint service, its list of patrons across the nation stood at 1,412. The WNU performed a heroic job during the wartime newsprint shortages and had to withstand, in the interest of fairness to all, many an impassioned plea for a larger order of readyprint sheets from publishers who found opportunities to increase their circulations during the wartime periods. The decision to abandon the readyprint phase of its business was attributed by the Western Newspaper Union partly to rising production costs, but mostly to a lessening demand for the service. "The recent emphasis on local news and only local news, as the key to success in a modern weekly, led more and more publishers to give up readyprint as soon as they were equipped to produce a full-sized local newspaper," an official of the company explained.[18] Discussions at state newspaper conventions around the country indicated that discontent with a lack of control over the advertising content, and a feeling that national advertising revenue which might otherwise come to the local papers was being drained off, were at least equally important reasons why publishers were dropping the readyprint service. Schools and departments of journalism had also been teaching their students that newspapers depending on readyprint were showing a lamentable lack of editorial vigor and news-gathering enterprise.

A Healthy Decline

Quite commonly, the decade 1910–20 is cited as the high point of the American weekly, with directories listing 16,850

[17] Thomas F. Barnhart, "The History of the Minnesota Editorial Association, 1867–1897" (Master's thesis, University of Minnesota, 1937).
[18] Farwell Perry, WNU president, as reported in The American Press, March, 1952.

in 1910. This figure went up past 17,000 at the mid-point of the decade. Yet even then it was recognized that these figures were inflated, as the following note makes clear:

Frank LeRoy Blanchard, editor of *Editor and Publisher*, New York: "According to Ayer's Directory, the total of all issues last year was 24,527, of which 17,323 were weeklies. After deducting all class, technical, social, scientific, literary, religious and other papers, we have left about 10,000 weeklies that are printed in the small cities and towns of the country."[19]

This supports the position that the American weekly newspaper's health hasn't been as precarious as the sharp decline in numbers would indicate. It does seem certain that directory statistics for the first two decades of this century were inflated by the presence of quite a number of newspapers which may have existed in name only, plus others which were intended to exist for just a limited time (certain political and "homestead" papers). Furthermore, there is the undeniable trend toward consolidation and merger, toward fewer but larger units, seen in almost all forms of business, not just the newspaper business. Political parties found access to other media of communication; they no longer desired to subsidize the papers which supported them (and long since had found that any hint a newspaper might be subsidized was positively detrimental both to it and the party which provided the subsidy). Editors, better trained and better qualified, prized their independence. Quite typical is the announcement of an editor taking over a new paper, stating that the policy would be politically independent, but that "we do not understand by it that easy-going neutrality which never dares say boo to a goose, and never has an opinion on any subject."[20]

Faster presses, powered by electric motors instead of gasoline engines or the still-earlier steam power, were able to produce editions for much larger circulations, giving added incentive to mergers. Introduction of new typesetting equipment coincidental with the changing nature of the labor supply, greatly changed the economics of publishing and encouraged the ever-larger unit. The application of a newer technology has not been universal, making generalizations of dubious value.

---

[19] *University of Missouri Bulletin—Journalism Series*, May, 1914.
[20] Joshua K. Bolles, *Father Was an Editor* (New York: W. W. Norton Co., 1940).

Even today the one-man shop, in which the publisher is his own editor, advertising salesman, printer, pressman, bookkeeper, mailer, and occasional janitor, may still be found, and the ads in the trade publications indicate the man-and-wife combination is considered a viable type of business enterprise. As of 1967 even the hand-set newspaper had not completely disappeared from the American scene.

At Last, the Local Focus

The changed attitude toward local news has been mentioned in several contexts. It is a little surprising, in light of the way we regard the weekly newspaper's function today, to note the comparatively brief span of time that the importance of local news has been recognized. An 86-year-old editor, attending a Florida state press convention in the 1930's, made the claim to be the "originator" of local news, although how he expected to be able to document such a claim in the face of the immense diversity of newspaper content in the eighteenth century is hard to imagine. It is true that the papers of the period prior to the Civil War had little or no local content. The average editor had no faith in the idea that his neighbors would pay for information they could obtain by word of mouth from their fellow townsfolk. A glance at old files of any section of the country shows that editors were likely to be notably deficient in their sense of news values. A typical example: "We learn from Westfield that on Sunday night last, a mill, which was also the residence of a family, was consumed by fire;—What renders this circumstance peculiarly distressing is, a man, his wife, and three children perished in the flames." No names, no details.

The editor of the Onondega (N. Y.) *Register* gave most of a column to a report of a "Great Fire at Mobile" (Alabama) while in the same issue he noted, in small type, an event in his own community two weeks after the event: "We have omitted to mention that the Store-house of Mr. John Rogers was destroyed by fire on the 6th inst. Mr. R's loss, we are sorry to add, is very considerable." The validity of the claim made by the octogenarian at the Florida convention is clouded by the remark of an eastern editor in 1827 that henceforth "a portion of our paper will, whenever expedient, be devoted to the local concerns and interests of this village."[21] Milton W. Hamilton's research into the country press of New York State discloses that the Cooperstown *Freeman's Journal* established a regular "local department" in 1851, but made no claim that it was an innovation.

California's first newspaper (1846), the *Californian,* followed the example of eastern contemporaries. Typical early issues showed several columns of "Pacific news," a second page composed largely of editorials and letters, a third page including a batch of news gleaned from Hawaiian papers and advertisements, the last page perhaps given over to a message from the mayor, news reprinted from Australian papers, or old eastern election returns. A great fire, said to be relatively equal in property destroyed and lives endangered to the 1906 San Francisco disaster, received a half-column, approximately 800 words.

[21] The three examples given are from Hamilton, *The Country Printer.*

Chapter 4

THE GREAT SHIFTS

THE BASIC REASONS for the decline in number and the changed attitudes toward weekly newspapers have been beyond any control of publishers or editors, whatever their intentions or capabilities. If the field which is the source of support is lost, the newspaper must die, just as a population of any kind will die if the food supply is removed or reduced below a certain minimum level. For the community newspaper the basic source of support is retail advertising; if the community is unable to sustain a viable retail shopping volume the newspaper can no longer exist except under exceptional circumstances.

As the appellation "rural weekly" indicates, by far the largest number of community newspapers has been closely tied to rural America. But that situation has been changing drastically in the last several decades. After figures for the 1960 U.S. Census had been compiled and published, Richard M. Scammon, then director of the Census Bureau, remarked, "Anybody who depends primarily on people for his business should be taking a good hard look at what is happening in these areas that are depopulating. The banker, the automobile dealer, the dentist, the soft-drink distributor—all these people have to bear in mind which way the population cat is going to jump."[1] Plainly it has jumped out of the rural areas into the urban centers. There is more than a little similarity between the community

---

[1] "Cities Crowding—Countryside Losing," *U.S. News & World Report*, May 7, 1962.

newspaper, often a family enterprise, and the family farm. Both are subjects of pious declarations by congressmen, state legislators, and many others in high places to the effect that their "values must be preserved," but forces which seem to be inexorable are working toward their reduction to a yet-to-be-determined minimum. Most remaining farms do become larger and financially more stable, just as many newspapers have merged into fewer but stronger units. For some types of business in the small town the fewer but larger farms may not mean a loss of sales volume—the larger farms may buy even more machinery, fertilizer, lumber, and general supplies. But the community newspaper has little hope of benefiting; the farmer, now occupying two or even three farms, still needs only one subscription, and since advertising volume is directly tied to circulation, the loss of rural population ordinarily is a serious blow for the weekly. The effect is cumulative. A Nebraska banker told a researcher, "Every time we lose ten to twelve average-sized farms in our trading area, we lose the purchasing power to sustain one business on Main Street."[2]

Many Small Papers Live On

In the eighteen midwestern farm states where the loss of rural population has been heaviest, a surprisingly large number of weekly newspapers still maintain existence in villages of 500 or less population. Minnesota may be taken as fairly typical of these states. Of the 319 nonsuburban and nonmetropolitan weekly and semi-weekly newspapers listed in the Minnesota Newspaper Association directory at the beginning of 1967, there were 37 published in villages of 500 or less. A whopping 93 more are published in towns of between 501 and 1,000 population. Some of the papers in quite small communities are not really independent units, but are owned by a neighboring publisher and printed in his plant, perhaps by substituting a nameplate and remaking front and back pages of his own paper. Random examination of directories shows many fewer weeklies in villages under 500 population in eastern, southern and far western states, and doubtless it would be relatively simple to

---

[2] *Ibid.*

trace reasons for this through the history of the way these regions were settled and their past and present economic conditions.

Professor Dwight A. Nesmith of Kansas State University,
director of a survey which studied more than 100 small towns in
Kansas, when asked about the future of the small town, replied
that the answer depends on a definition of the term. "If you're
talking about towns of less than 2,500, located outside the orbit
of a metropolitan area that is growing, the answer is relatively
simple. I think the handwriting is on the wall for a good many
of these towns. . . . The 'problem' towns are the agricultural-
service communities that were scattered so liberally over the
Missouri Basin by land speculators and railroad-stock salesmen
in the frontier days. It's not a popular thing to say, but the
people in rural areas will be better off if many of these towns
are allowed to die."[3]

Other rural sociologists and agricultural economists put
the critical level at 1,000 population, but all are careful to point
out that communities are as varied as the human organism in
responses to environment, that some show amazing vitality under the most difficult conditions, whereas others more favorably
situated, and perhaps larger to start with, do decline. Unex-
pected infusions may restore vigor—an industry may decide to
build a plant in or near a small village, guaranteeing an additional population of several hundred, plus the service trades
and small businesses which such an increase will attract; an oil
or mining development may tap new resources for an area; the
Defense Department may relocate a base. These are the exceptions, and serve largely to point up the truth of the general
statements made about the continuing decline of small villages.

All right, the population is increasing sharply every year—
where do the people live? Not necessarily in the big cities.
They move to nearby trading centers of 5,000 or more population, or to the suburbs of the metropolitan areas. The Upper
Midwest Research and Development Council issued a report on
migration and population growth which predicted that an increasing share of rural migrants can be expected to remain in
the region's cities. This five-state, heavily agricultural region
had a population gain of approximately 500,000 during the
1950's but would have grown another 392,000 had it not been

---

[3] *Ibid.*

for net migration losses; the urban in-migration of 190,000 was offset by the rural out-migration of 582,000. The report commented that other areas of the country have greater problems than the Upper Midwest, that "many other areas are finding a decline also in their urban areas . . . we do not have a picture of over-all decline, but one of an adjustment process."[4]

Small Retailers Suffer

If the small town and village are largely agricultural-service communities, and the people they service move away, the resulting effect on their retail businesses must be obvious. Many editors have commented, bitterly if their political orientation was strong, on the effect of the government's soil bank programs. They said many farm couples, in late middle age with their children perhaps grown and gone, decide to "retire" early, put a major portion of the farm in the soil bank, rent out the rest, and move to town (or perhaps to California or Florida). Others, nowhere near retirement age, may decide to outwait a period of low farm prices by putting the farm in the soil bank and moving to a town or city to take jobs. The jobs often aren't available in the village or small town; they may be in nearby cities of 10,000–25,000. These families may fully intend to return to farming, and it is conceivable that in the predicted periods of food scarcity for a ballooning population they will, but many will find the challenge of reassembling machinery and equipment and of adapting to rapidly changing production methods just too discouraging, and their current situations too comfortable, to go back. The land hunger of their neighbors who stayed will do the rest; the owners will sell their land to the resident farmers who must increase their acreage to maximize their efficiency. Better equipment, better methods, increased use of power, improved soil management permit the individual on the farm today to accomplish immeasurably more than his forefathers did in longer working days. Roswell Garst, the Iowa farmer who shot into international prominence as one of the hosts of former Soviet Premier Nikita Khrushchev on his visit to the United States, uses a graphic illustration of the

[4] Russell B. Adams, *Population Mobility* (Upper Midwest Economic Study for Upper Midwest Research and Development Council, June, 1964).

changes: "When I started farming in 1916 it took an American farmer about 30 minutes of labor to raise a bushel of corn. Now the average cornbelt farmer raises a bushel of corn in something like five minutes, and the really alert ones in something like 2½ minutes."[5]

These are just some of the reasons for the rural migration, all of them having significance for the eventual changes which must come about in the weekly newspaper field. No one should expect revolutionary developments. Like their little communities, many small newspaper operations have great vitality and staying power. One of the most striking examples is seen in this letter published about eight years ago in the *Kansas Publisher,* monthly magazine of the Kansas Press Association:

You will find attached a clipping from the February *Publisher.* I am writing this to bring you up to date on your "hand-set" information. (Ed. note: quoting from the clipping—"re Winchester Star—the Star is one of the few remaining hand-set papers in the country and is thought to be the only one in Kansas at the present time.")

The Sawyer News was established in 1907. It has been under my wife's and my ownership since 1934. The News has always been and is still a handset paper. And it is a paying paper. I have never yet been able to persuade my income tax computer that I did not make enough to exempt me from some income tax. Out of date perhaps—but since 1934 the paper paid off $5,000 debts acquired trying to farm. Also put a daughter through the University, bought a quarter of block here with home on it, and—oh well, I am bragging now, but a little handset paper can still exist and keep its owner. Of course, it takes long hours and hard work. But we like it. We have over twice as many paid subs as is the population of Sawyer, which is not many, of course. Job work keeps us swamped. So *don't* let them kid you, that a little handset paper can't exist and the editor and his wife have a lot of fun publishing it. Thanks for your time if you have read this far.

                              (Signed) BYRON E. BLAIR AND HIS
                                              HARD-WORKING WIFE.
                              Sawyer, Kansas

A case can be made for the assertion that a lively, progressive newspaper can either "save" a deteriorating village or turn a decline around. It would need community support, but just one or two other forceful, progressive merchants might provide the necessary push. The editor of a market letter for a hard-

---

[5] *U.S. News & World Report,* May 7, 1962.

ware association discussed the pessimistic view of the small town taken by many of the association members. "I can think of one situation," he wrote, "where the town by all rights, reason, and statistics, should have faded out of the picture long ago. Yet today they are healthy and developing their potential. In this small town the hardware store is doing a volume of over $200,000 annually, making a substantial net profit, and growing year after year. Why? This store is as modern and up-to-date as any store in the state. Their merchandise is attractive, well balanced, and suited to their customers' needs and wants. They utilize all the promotional and advertising helps available to bring and keep their customers in their town. . . . This town and many like it are not fading out of the picture because they have recognized their problems and are taking the necessary action to keep their store and community healthy."[6] There are examples of weekly newspapers which resemble that hardware store in that they aggressively reach out beyond what might be regarded as their natural field to build circulation and to attract more advertisers. These papers will undoubtedly last many years, or at least while they are operated by their present publishers.

War is Hell on Papers, Too

Dislocations caused by the two world wars, the Korean conflict, and to a much lesser extent the Viet Nam action, had a great "shake-out" effect on weekly newspapers. This was especially true in World War II when the tremendous manpower demands both of the armed forces and the war industries forced the suspension of hundreds of weekly newspapers across the nation. Under special laws protecting the legality of these suspended papers, quite a number were revived in 1946–47, but a majority were naturally marginal operations at best and they stayed dead.

Newsprint, labor, and supply costs shot up in the postwar period, making all the more discouraging the task of breathing new life into these moribund newspapers. It was simpler and more remunerative for potential publishers to work for some-

[6] Henry J. Parsinen, *Market Letter* (distributed by Our Own Hardware, buying cooperative for independent retailers, July, 1961).

one else. Instead of the widely predicted slump in employment in the conversion to peace-time activity, instead of Henry Wallace's goal of "Sixty Million Jobs" remaining wildly visionary, the demand for manpower remained strong. Young men who might have made the sacrifice involved in becoming proprietors found incentives which made other positions more attractive; some who did return to the publishing field or entered it for the first time found it too difficult to find or retain employees, and so dropped the papers again.

Speakers at state press association meetings after World War II expressed strong hopes for the future of the field through an influx of college-trained editors. The huge increase in college enrollments under the GI Bill did provide a source of supply, but the influx never really materialized to the extent envisioned because no constructive methods of financing young people, either to revive suspended papers or buy and modernize existing ones, appeared. Short-term credit was readily available, to be sure, but if the loan was to be of any size, a repayment schedule based on 36 months, or even 60 months, usually made the amortized payments too large for the income of the business when they were superimposed on other obligations. And the loans had to be sizeable in a period when a new typesetting machine cost $12,000 or a used one perhaps $5,000, when a much-used flatbed press capable of printing four eight-column pages at one impression might cost $3,000, and other equipment was priced proportionately.

Purchase of a paper was not as simple as testimony has indicated it might have been "in the old days." A prudent seller had better get enough of a down payment to assure that the buyer has an equity sufficient to assure that he won't just simply walk away when the going gets a little tough, as so many home-buyers have done in periods of easy financing. The federal income tax laws in regard to capital gains made the figure of 29 per cent of the sale price a customary requirement. Thus a young man, perhaps an ex-GI hoping to realize an ambition to be independent, to serve society in the role of an editor and publisher, usually found it difficult to raise the capital required for a down payment of 25 to 29 per cent of the purchase price. A rough rule-of-thumb used in this period stated that a weekly newspaper ought to be worth an average of its annual gross over a period of three to five years, plus or minus a percentage depending on other factors. Even papers in under-500 villages might gross $30,000, and thus $7,500 to $10,000 might be required for a down payment, in addition to which the purchaser had better be sure he had adequate operating capital for half a year or so.

The postwar period had quite a turnover among small papers, and one substantial reason was the surprising way so many small papers survived the shake-out. A study made in 1958 showed, for instance, that of Nebraska's 261 nonmetropolitan weeklies, 60 were being published in villages of 500 or less population; Kansas had 48 of its 309 weekly and semi-weekly newspapers in under-500 communities; Iowa had 48 of 404 in the under-500 class; Minnesota had 56 of 362 weeklies and semi-weeklies classified as "rural" which were being published in villages under 500; and Illinois had 48 of its complete total at that time of 656 weeklies, semi-weeklies, and tri-weeklies (but many of these were suburban).[7] Throughout the late '50's and so far into the '60's each of these states continued to show a slow decline in the number of rural weeklies, and almost invariably the casualties were in the villages of under 1,000 population. Some of these papers had been taken over by young publishers who later just gave up the struggle, deciding it would be wiser to abandon their equity and close the paper rather than devote any more of their lives to these projects. Young editors who had been forced into long hours of struggle with antiquated equipment, with no time left for the editorials and in-depth news stories they longed to write, quickly became disillusioned and moved into urban journalism or left the field of journalism altogether.

Some Are Disillusioned

Some felt a lack of satisfaction even when they were not burdened with the responsibilities of management, when they might just have been "trying out" the field. Henry Beetle Hough, the noted country editor whose books about his experiences in running a weekly newspaper have been widely popular, observed:

---

[7] John Cameron Sim, "Weekly Newspapers Again Facing Challenge to Move," *Journalism Quarterly*, Spring, 1958.

. . . these young people, fledgling reporters, really wanted a story-book kind of experience that did not exist. . . . They will read in the paper the things they themselves have written but they can-not be expected to read the rest of the paper or to be interested in the ways and processes by which the community functions, or in much of anything that does not impinge upon their own careers. They will be passionately concerned with the plight of races and nations overseas, but they cannot understand and do not care to understand why Bill Smith belongs to a lodge and what he gets out of it. If he lived in Abyssinia, his case would fascinate them and they would be his passionate advocates, but he happens to be just a home-town guy in America. Deadlines are mystic . . . ap-parently [the reporter] believes that when the copy leaves his hands the important function is completed and all else is virtually automatic.[8]

There's a deceptive aspect to the apparent health of some small communities, at least insofar as a publisher may be con-cerned. The village may be holding its population, or even gaining, but it could be less and less desirable as a field for a weekly newspaper. The statement about the necessity of a good base for retail advertising must be reiterated here at a risk of laboring the point, but it must be understood that a village may be gaining population even while it is losing its retail business. The growing ease and popularity of what may be called "rural commuting" is responsible. This is not to be confused with the stereotype of the white-collar executive tak-ing a train to the city to spend the day in a skyscraper office building. It is more a picture of a blue-collar or clerical work-er who drives to the factory job, school, or office. He may be a part-time farmer. A report on population mobility for the Upper Midwest Research and Development Council says:

It is a form of daily mobility which can be a substitute for a resi-dential move closer to one's job. Work trips have greatly length-ened and increased in numbers from suburban and outlying areas to places of employment. The labor force has grown by 50 percent and the number of cars on the road has more than doubled since 1950. . . . The desire for open space, the phenomenal rise in auto ownership, and reduced highway travel time have been the stim-ulants to commuting. Hundreds of small towns and rural town-ships have entered the employment orbit of larger centers. About 40 percent of the region's small towns lie within 50 miles of an urban area having 10,000 population or more. . . . The trend is

---

[8] *Once More the Thunderer* (New York, Ives Washburn, 1950).

making it possible for many communities, formerly dependent upon farm trade, to hold their own, and even grow.[9]

From the view of the sociologist or economist, a good case can be made for transformation of small towns into "satellite" communities because they have a number of inherent advantages: plenty of low-cost space, existing housing, public facilities, and salutary family living conditions. Adams suggests that encouragement of home-to-work commuting from small towns and rural areas to growing centers would yield dividends both to employers and to under-employed workers. This same mobility for employment can be extended, however, to the family's buying practices. The location of shopping centers and discount stores offering a complete range of retail goods and services at the outskirts of urban centers makes it all the more convenient for the blue-collar commuter and members of his family to do most of their purchasing outside of the town in which they reside. The impact is felt first by the general or department store and by the local groceries. They are forced out of business, and with them goes the bulk of a small weekly newspaper's ad linage. The town retains many of the smaller stores and service establishments, but these serve mostly the fringe and emergency needs of the residents. The stores disclaim need for any extensive advertising program, and probably they are right. If the small town has had its infusion of new population vigor because a manufacturing plant of some kind locates there, this may not greatly change the picture for local retail business. The company itself has little need for the kind of supplies the small retailer can provide, and the employees still have the mobility which enables them to shop at nearby urban centers even though the workers are no longer required to commute. Competition for the small town merchant is just too tough, and it promises to be tougher. Hear Martin B. Kohn, president of the National Retail Merchants Association, in an address to members of his association in May, 1966:

Migration to the suburbs *and beyond the suburbs* [emphasis added] will continue. New shopping centers—larger than ever—are being and will be built. The one big store center is out-dated; two, three, and four department stores will be in single, large regional centers. Our stores will be where the customers want them. And not only

---

[9] Adams, *Population Mobility*.

powerful suburban stores—there will be, in addition to the usual
specialty and service stores, TWIGS—department store specialty
shops—furniture twigs, casual dress twigs, shoe twigs, etc. . . . The
decline of downtown business has stopped in most [urban] communities. Stores have been modernized and a few new stores have
been built. The hub of the city is where the excitement—the entertainment takes place, and it is our prediction that there will be
increased business in our downtown areas. We believe all kinds of
competition will continue to grow. More and more outlets of all
kinds, whether they be supermarkets, gas stations, or routemen, will
sell soft goods. Notice the new buildings of the discount, mail order
and variety chains; the stark, poorly designed outlets have disappeared. They have learned from us and we have learned from
them—something about unit pricing as opposed to average mark-up,
self-selection fixtures that display merchandise more attractively
and even, in some cases, check-out selling. We look for current
distinctions within the retail mix to be less apparent.[10]

Competition of the "Shopper"

The extension "beyond the suburbs" suggested by Mr.
Kohn brings many shopping centers into or adjacent to small
towns. Does that not then guarantee a good advertising volume
for the small town publisher? Not necessarily; in fact, rather
seldom. These operations are predicated on mass volume;
they handle their advertising in the same way. They want
saturation coverage of an area, and this is seldom provided by
the weekly newspaper even in its own field, and that field is
likely to be much more constricted than the shopping center's
trade territory. The blanket coverage CAN be provided by a
"shopper," which has the format of a newspaper, handles its
display advertising like a newspaper, may even run news like a
newspaper, but which fails under the ordinary definitions of
newspaper because it has no paid circulation—to attain that
saturation coverage it must be distributed free. Some alert publishers in towns taken over by shopping center merchandising
have met the challenge by combining the concepts of shopper
and newspaper, issuing both. Then, because the pervasive
effect of radio and television is not limited to urban areas, we
find the merchants of even small, rather isolated communities
demanding from the print medium the same blanket coverage

---

[10] "A Retailer Looks at Change," *Editor & Publisher*, May 28, 1966.

they think they get from radio, and they want shoppers printed for their limited trade areas. As a result many publishers in small villages, or in larger towns which have become "bedroom" communities without much retail business, have been able by printing shoppers to maintain or increase their advertising revenues enough to sustain thriving weekly newspapers. This takes aggressiveness, requires application of principles of good management, and means increased investment in efficient equipment or processes. Publishers deficient in these (or perhaps even one of these) requirements have been those whose newspapers have been failing. Some who are too old to make the effort, or who are too entrenched in their ways to desire to change, will continue to publish for some years (we have noted in several contexts the seemingly unquenchable vitality of little papers) and then they will be the ones noted in some future year-end casualty lists compiled by state press association managers.

A Fateful Prognosis

The wistful wish, "If only we could build up the town's population," would not always bring a happy solution. Albert W. Allar of the Smithtown (N.Y.) *Messenger* points out that his county (Suffolk on Long Island) is the fastest-growing in the nation; population leaped from 275,000 in 1950 to more than 700,000 in the mid-1960's. "Ironically, I don't think there's a single weekly newspaper publisher in the county who is happy about it," he said. "With population saturation came the big department stores and the chain grocery markets. They require mass circulation media to compete for the consumer's shrinking dollar."[11] He could have added that big dailies come in, too.

Does all this add up to an excessively gloomy picture for the community weekly? Only for the weak weekly in a weak village. The figures cited in this chapter show that in some states a quarter of the weekly papers, in other states up to a third of them, are in hamlets, villages, or small towns which have only bleak prospects for survival. These towns won't be

---

[11] "How to Compete With Other Media in Growing Suburbs," *New York Weekly Press*, Syracuse, January, 1963.

abandoned, buildings will remain, and so will a number of residents, but they won't have the economic strength to support a newspaper. But if we grant that such losses are inevitable in the next decade it still leaves between two-thirds and three-quarters of the newspapers in communities which really should grow larger because of the general population increase and because of the considerable trend to decentralization fed by dissatisfaction with the big city's intolerable conditions of air and water pollution, street crime, traffic jams, and slum ugliness.

In contrast to these anticipated losses there will be the gains from the trend examined at length in the latter part of this book—the thriving suburban weekly press. To some extent it has grown by a form of accretion, in which the suburbs creep out from the metropolitan center to engulf formerly separate communities. Their "rural" newspapers then fell into the new classification of suburban, often to the dismay of the new breed of aggressive publishers who thought that the outdated product in their midst scarred the bright image they wanted to show for big advertisers.

Indeed, for the weekly press as a whole, suburban or "hometown," the disappearance of these marginal operations, poorly printed, without editorials, erratic in news coverage, filling space with publicity blurbs, has to be an advantage, much as one may sympathize with the little community which loses its "own" paper. If one serves as a judge in state newspaper contests, as the author has, he will surely be impressed (and distressed) at the ease and speed with which literally scores of newspapers can be immediately tossed out of consideration for any common category—news, editorials, features, pictures, advertising. Too many of these poorly run papers have persisted well beyond their time, and they now do little more than contribute to the stereotype image (fostered even by some recent documentary television programs) held by much of the American public of the weekly newspaper as a laughable old relic filled with trivia.

Chapter 5

THE GREAT NEW "THIRD FORCE"

MANY OF THE REASONS cited for the decline of the press in the heavily rural areas of the nation are the factors, in reverse, which have contributed to the explosive growth of suburban weeklies and dailies in the past two decades. The development has been impressive enough to justify recognition of the suburban weekly as a distinctive type of print media journalism justifying the appellation of "The Third Force." This self-awareness frequently gives the impression that here is indeed a new development, yet there are references more than a half-century old which show that publishers of newspapers in big-city areas felt they had problems not shared by other weeklies. *The History of the Illinois Press Association* has a note from the minutes of the 1914 meeting: "The Suburban [Chicago] Publishers Association was organized in this year, with Ray Peacock of the Jefferson Park *Jeffersonian* as president. The organization was an outgrowth of the old Cook County Press Association. Thirty publishers attended the first meeting which was held at the Morrison hotel."[1]

This feeling of separateness (which has resulted in many attempts at separate organizations culminating in establishment of a separate suburban section of the National Newspaper Association [NNA] in 1966) was recognized in the pioneering study, *The Suburban Weekly*, by Margaret V. Cosse at Columbia Uni-

---

[1] H. L. Williamson, *History of the Illinois Press Association* (Springfield: Hartman-Jefferson Printing Co., 1934).

63

versity in 1928. She said, in describing the nature of her research, that, "From this, one may conclude only that the suburban weekly is a highly individualized newspaper, extremely diverse in its nature, and that, since it is a comparatively new development in journalism, no generalizations can be made that will apply to all suburban weeklies . . . a highly specialized socializing force." This cogent statement is even truer today; generalizations about this volatile field are indeed unsafe. The tremendous diversity of these papers in size, appearance, content, format, production methods, and statements of purpose may exceed even the range of differences in their country cousins, if only because their fields can be so markedly different. Miss Cosse displayed considerable perspicacity when she concluded:

To predict what may or may not take place in the future is mere speculation. So with the suburban weekly. But one can safely say there will always be the suburban weekly as long as there is the great metropolitan daily. . . . And as the present metropolitan units double their areas through annexation of various suburban communities, the journalistic situation will not be changed. For, while some suburban weeklies may perish in the process of absorption, others will spring up in what will then be the new suburban territory. As new communities are developed, new community newspapers will be founded. They are an integral part of local life . . . will set standards for the operation of weekly newspapers that will cause their rural neighbors to throw off their bucolic mannerisms for more practical methods.[2]

This predicted effect has certainly been felt, even if it has not eliminated "bucolic mannerisms." The few front-runners in the suburban field were not followed even by the mass of their contemporaries. Most continued, indeed, to pattern themselves as closely as they could after leading rural weeklies and to boast that they served the same functions—that they were "billboards," that they were holding a mirror up to the community, that they provided an economically feasible advertising medium for merchants and customers of a well-defined geographical area. Indeed, at the time Miss Cosse wrote (1927–28) she believed, "The man who contents himself with the suburban weekly is generally not a journalist of the highest type.

---

[2] *The Suburban Weekly* (New York: Columbia University Press, 1928).

Why, one cannot say. His training, however, is mediocre, and his latent ability not much better. This may also be true of the younger men and women in rural and metropolitan journalism, but it is doubtful . . . perhaps it is because the importance of the suburban weekly and its possibilities for development have not been fully realized."

Now It's Maturing

Edwin G. Schwenn, who prepared a series on "The Press in Suburbia" for the *Publishers' Auxiliary* in the summer of 1961, felt the real change could be pinpointed in the great population shifts in and following World War II:

The medium, taken as a whole, is comparatively young, born out of and to fill a need caused by the population explosion of the late forties and fifties. . . . The medium, of course, has its older elements, the newspapers thirty or more years old which have had to change their editorial and advertising function to expand with their communities. Those that survived in these areas during the growth period prospered, and are essentially much different than they were before their area's population growth.[3]

This self-awareness of their unique opportunities caused some of the leading publishers in the field to form the Suburban Press Foundation, Incorporated, which has its executive office in Chicago. The best papers had long demonstrated how effective they could be in choosing a role where the metropolitan dailies really could not compete, in anticipating social, economic, and political problems in their communities, covering the news in these developments in depth and commenting editorially with clarity and vigor. Yet their success did not mean that all papers in all suburbs immediately fell in behind them, using the best of their methods, any more than the great mass of community weeklies ever applied the practices demonstrated to be successful by contest prize-winners over a period of decades.

Dr. Curtis D. MacDougall, professor of journalism at

---

[3] *The Press in Suburbia* (pamphlet reprint of series from *Publishers' Auxiliary* [July 22 – October 7, 1961]).

Northwestern University, who served as a consultant for the
Suburban Press Foundation for a period after its founding,
recognized a basic reason for this lag:

The main obstacle . . . is the inveterate difficulty humans have
of breaking old habits. Most suburban publishers who feel they
are falling short of full realization of their potentialities would admit, if they could start from scratch, they would not put out the
kind of papers they now do. How, however, to get out of the rut
today? Old publishers, old editors, old publishers' wives and editors'
wives, old cronies about town are "sot" in their ways. Those ways
may add up to a product which is not much more than a journalistic bulletin board . . . the news story of the meeting of the village
board or the city council and the half-dozen or so local items re-
garding unusual arrests and automobile accidents. . . . A blind
spot which suburban publishers share with their metropolitan
counterparts is inability to recognize the necessity for increased costs
of newsgathering. Most suburban newspapers do not cover the
news of their communities, and, in many instances, are not even
aware of much or most of what is going on. They do not go out
in search of news; they merely accept and print virtually unchanged
whatever is submitted to them. . . . Those suburban publishers
who persist in their refusal to augment their news staffs . . . are
going to get run out of town by new competitors who will econo-
mize on production methods in order to reap the news harvest that
is available.[4]

The new production methods were also largely postwar
developments, at least to the extent that they became economically feasible for weekly publishers. Several big companies
plunged into a race for development of a relatively inexpensive
web-fed offset press; others sought to develop cheaper composition methods suited to the offset process which would eliminate,
or reduce the importance of, typesetting machines using slugs
set from molten metal. The large investments required for this
new equipment (which also had decidedly greater capacity)
pushed publishers toward multiple-ownership concepts or centralized printing facilities for separately owned units. Schwenn
found that of 387 publishers answering his question "Do you
publish more than one newspaper?" 44 per cent said they did,
and that they averaged 2.8 newspapers each. Schwenn said the
trend appeared definitely to be upward and guessed that by
1970 the three-paper average for multiple publishers will be
"considerably higher."[5] Events since 1961 have fully borne out

[4] *Ibid.*
[5] *Ibid.*

the prediction. Groups and chains have been active both in starting new papers where builders and developers have created new communities, and they have also absorbed many independent newspaper operations. Groups of twenty-five or more may be found in several sections of the country.

Audiences Offer Potential

Several basic advantages reinforce the trend which shows the number of suburban newspapers increasing while the number of other community papers declines. Though the suburban editor often complains that his community is frustratingly diffuse and scattered, his audience is still much more concentrated than that of the average rural weekly. This enables many suburban newspapers to use a carrier system, which becomes all the more desirable as second class postage rates continue to go up. The carrier can be a circulation builder; no method of subscription selling has been found as effective as face-to-face presentations, and even the youthful, inexperienced, stumbling carrier salesman is likely to be a more potent sales force than a letter or a radio commercial.

The suburban newspaper's audience can be touted as homogeneous, possessing higher-than-average income and education levels, and compact enough to justify selling advertisers on the advantage of the "rifle-shot" technique over the "scatter-gun"; i.e. advertising to a specialized audience versus the mass audience. The quality audience will justify higher advertising rates than most nonsuburban weeklies ever dare to think of charging; this in turn provides the greater economic strength which enables the suburban publisher to be more progressive in his choice and use of efficient modern equipment. He can also, theoretically at least, attract better qualified editorial and advertising staff members by paying better salaries; indeed, he must compete on relatively even terms with the metropolitan media.

The metropolitans have evinced growing concern with their suburban competition for nearly two decades now. The cries of alarm rose to a crescendo when consolidation reduced the number of downtown dailies in Los Angeles from four to two; the numerous suburban papers, daily and weekly, in the

Los Angeles area were said to provide too much competition. In an interview given to *Editor & Publisher* in 1958, Maurice Fischer, then city editor of the Chicago *Daily News*, was quoted to the effect that he believed the biggest local competitors of metropolitan dailies are the community weeklies "within the city and in suburban towns. The community press is much more a direct competitor at the local level than are radio and television. . . . Some of our community papers are excellent today. Many of them are getting better all the time. Community papers have gotten fat as a result of the population growth in the outlying suburban areas of big cities. Metropolitan papers, in turn, find it necessary to have zoned suburban sections and to provide increased 'local' coverage of important community affairs. Nothing is news until it is local."[6]

This device of zoned editions to provide that "local" news of the suburbs has been and is being used in virtually every major city where there is an extensive suburban press. Naturally the mets' concern is not primarily that some important news sector will go uncovered, but rather that too much ad revenue is being siphoned off by the burgeoning suburbans. The zoned editions provide a way of reducing the waste circulation which an advertiser serving a limited geographical area would otherwise have to buy whenever he advertised in the metropolitan daily. He can get his advertising at a rate commensurate with the size of the audience which really will have some opportunity of visiting, or at least passing by, his store. Wherever the zoned editions were started they were likely to occasion cries of alarm from the suburbans in their turn. The following excerpts were typical of the initial reaction:

And so now comes the searching for advertising accounts that have long been the backbone of the weekly press. The tentacles are reaching out, and attached are signs of "greater coverage," "low prices," and more suburban news. . . . The battle lines have been drawn, and the Suburban press is united in its efforts against the octopus of domination.[7]
. . . designed apparently to wean advertisers away from the weeklies and result, eventually, in the same fate for the weeklies that befell [other discontinued papers]. . . . As to the ethics of the zone circulation plan, we are most dubious. The weekly press has always

---

[6] George A. Brandenburg, "Need Reporters Who Report and Write," *Editor & Publisher,* November 29, 1958.
[7] *Anoka* (Minn.) *County Union,* October 11, 1957.

championed competition as the life-blood of democracy, but if the zone circulation program's ultimate objective is, as it seems to be, the merciless crushing and elimination of weekly newspapers regardless of cost, it certainly cannot be termed fair competition. Our battle plans in this "war" are simple: We will continue to work as hard as possible to give [our city] the best newspaper within our capacity.[8]

This latter solution proved to be, of course, the most effective, as it would be for any enterprise involved in a highly competitive situation. Both sides soon found that some earlier fears were exaggerated and that both could adjust in a way which really was of the greatest benefit both to readers and to advertisers. Norman Chandler, publisher of the Los Angeles *Times,* speaking to the 1959 convention of the American Society of Newspaper Editors, said he expected to see more than the 28 evening papers then published in suburbs within 60 miles of downtown Los Angeles and that he would not be perturbed by the development: "A large paper cannot compete with them and they ought to do very well in the future." Roy Roberts, then editor of the Kansas City *Star,* agreed that the number of suburban competitors could be expected to increase, and offered the prescription which has proved to be so healing for both sides—"Nothing wins like getting out a good newspaper."[9]

In the mid-1960's there was startling evidence that the metropolitans were coming around to an adage long honored in competitive fields: "If you can't beat 'em, join 'em." A headline in a trade publication in June, 1966, described a development which was neither the first of its kind nor the most extensive:

Zone editions didn't work so . . .
TORONTO'S TELEGRAM
ACQUIRES FIVE
EXURBAN WEEKLIES

The story quoted an announcement letter sent out by the *Telegram* and singled out this paragraph which it put in italics:

---

[8] Richfield (Minn.) *News,* October 9, 1957.
[9] Chandler and Roberts comments from ASNE Convention reported in "Suburban Papers Grow, 'Mets' Decline, ASNE Told," *Editor & Publisher,* April 18, 1959.

"The regions around Metro are expanding at a rapid rate and offer a rich market to any advertiser. *They can be most effectively reached through the medium of the local newspaper, which generates high reader interest through local news coverage.*" The article said that the *Telegram* had tried zoned editions for about two years prior to a strike in 1963, then had not reinstated the editions when publication resumed after the strike.[10]

About the same time the Gannett Company, publisher of a group of daily newspapers, announced purchase of the ten weekly papers produced under the name of Suburban Newspaper Group of Cherry Hill, N.J. William A. Stretch, a Gannett director, was quoted in *The Jersey Publisher* as saying "Expansion of the Gannett organization into the weekly newspaper field in South Jersey is part of a policy of maintaining the best possible public service and coverage of home-town news in a growing community. Even more than a metropolitan daily, a weekly can provide a detailed account of the news in its own neighborhood."[11]

The Scripps-Howard chain announced in the spring of 1965 that it had entered the weekly newspaper field with the purchase of the Stuart (Fla.) *News,* a prize-winning paper with a circulation of 4,860. Earlier the Chicago *Tribune* purchased a couple of small city newspapers in areas far removed from its own territory.

Late in 1966 the newspaper group headed by Ralph Ingersoll, the one-time publisher of *Time* magazine and later founder of the experimental newspaper *PM* in New York City, bought a group of six weeklies in the Philadelphia suburban area. One of the group, the *News of Delaware* in Upper Darby, has claimed the largest paid circulation of any weekly of general distribution, with something in excess of 32,000.

Another aspect of the interest a daily might show in weeklies was demonstrated in 1966 when, as one of the steps in preparing to publish a new daily, the Suffolk (N.Y.) *Sun,* Cowles Communications, Inc., purchased three Suffolk weekly papers, half of the chain published by Sunrise Press, Inc. The three weeklies were intended to provide a circulation spring-

      [10] "Toronto Telegram Acquires Five Exurban Weeklies," *The American Press,* June, 1966.
      [11] Gannett Company Purchases 10 Suburban Group Weeklies," *The Jersey Publisher,* June, 1966.

board for the new daily, which bought the publishing rights and circulation lists, but no physical plants.

The apprehension expressed by some weekly publishers upon the introduction of zoned edition competition was mild compared to that aroused when Field Enterprises, Inc., which includes the Chicago *Daily News* and *Sun-Times* among its properties, introduced the *Arlington Day,* a new daily for the Chicago suburb of Arlington Heights, on January 31, 1966. A rumor that this was only the first of a group of such dailies seemed to be confirmed when the *Prospect Day* began publishing April 18, 1966, in Prospect Heights, and even more disturbing to weekly publishers was the comment of John Stanton, editor of *Arlington Day,* that he had "received calls from other metropolitan editors and publishers over the country who read into this move their own pet plan."[12] That Field Enterprises intended to take a full swing at this venture into the suburbs was indicated when construction began in May, 1966, on a new $2,000,000 offset printing plant in suburban Elk Grove Village to produce the two *Days,* a shopper, and outside contract printing.

The Shopper Bogeyman

It was really the shopper which gave weekly publishers their greatest uneasiness. They could speak with some confidence of competing in the news field with new dailies, but shoppers have been the bane of newspapers since the great depression of the 1930's. Publishers believe there is a limited amount of advertising revenue in any one area—the sum of all the advertising budgets of all the businesses—and that the more competitors there are for the advertising dollar, the thinner the slice for each, or else some of the contestants drive others out. They have learned pretty well how to compete with the broadcast media, trade publications, or direct mail, but a shopper is another print medium very much like the newspaper, and the arguments successful against the other media may often boomerang when applied to the shopper.

When the *Arlington Day* began publication as a five-day

---

[12] "New Day in Suburban Publishing," *The American Press,* February, 1966.

(Monday through Friday) daily, it was accompanied by *Market Day*, published on Thursdays and distributed free to 57,000 homes. It might appear at first glance that the *Day* was competing against itself with *Market Day*, but experience has shown over the years that the most effective lifesaver for a newspaper threatened by an independent shopper ("Typhoid Mary" some newspapermen bitterly call it) is for the newspaper to print its own and offer some form of combination rates for the two publications.

In starting with both its daily newspaper and a free distribution shopper, Field Enterprises was engaging its direct competition on all fronts. Apparently there had been no probing for weak spots; on the face of it Field executives had decided to give this new enterprise the most rugged test possible, and in entering Arlington Heights they were confronting a suburban newspaper operation widely recognized as one of the strongest, most progressive in the country. This is Paddock Publications, which has published a paper in Arlington Heights for more than seventy years, and which has been publishing papers for fifteen surrounding suburban communities: Addison, Bensenville, Elk Grove Village, Hoffman Estates, Itasca, Mount Prospect, Palatine, Prospect Heights, Rolling Meadows, Roselle, Wheeling, Hanover-Streamwood, and the *Du Page County Register*, and *Cook County Herald*. Furthermore, Paddock was printing a shopper, the *Sunday Suburbanite*, for all these communities, offering 71,000 circulation. It may be called a shopper in that distribution is free, but Stuart R. Paddock, co-publisher and editor emeritus, explained that it really resembled a newspaper because of the amount of news and features carried, much of it picked up from the sixteen regular newspapers but some prepared especially for the Sunday edition when the time element in the news made it necessary.

Paddock Fights Back. Through a series of building and expansion programs in the past decade, the latest in 1965, the Paddock firm was in a good position to meet the threat, and moved vigorously to put into effect plans for improving news coverage and modernizing editorial and advertising layout. Then, at the beginning of 1967 the officers of the Paddock firm—Stuart R. Paddock, Sr., and Charles S. Paddock, co-publishers; Stuart R. Paddock, Jr., and Robert Y. Paddock, vice presidents—were hosts at a luncheon for suburban officials and civic leaders at which they announced plans for a publication schedule which would in effect give the area tri-weekly newspapers (not a big time lag from a five-day daily). Effective March 1, the weekly editions of the sixteen papers and the Sunday shopper were discontinued as such, to be replaced by publications dated Wednesday, Friday, and Sunday. Robert Paddock told the group that the tri-weekly schedule was intended to offer more compact, better organized (through more intensive departmentalization) papers; increased timeliness in news and photo coverage but at no sacrifice of in-depth treatment of news; more editorial comment and news analysis; increased attention to sports news and to material reflecting the interests of teen-agers and young adults.[13]

Publishers React.[14] When the plans for the *Arlington Day* were announced, a meeting of the Cook County Suburban Publishers association was convened, with 35 publishers, representing more than 120 weeklies, attending. Claude Walker, editor of the Forest Park *Review* and secretary of the association, told an interviewer for the trade press that most members were concerned that the venture represented a master plan under which many suburban communities will be picked as sites for new dailies. In this event, Walker said bravely, "We'll just get out a better product. We think it can be a healthy thing for all of us. . . . We should cooperate with each other more effectively. . . . We have the know-how to put out a more interesting product." Charles Hayes, executive editor for Paddock Publications, said the more interesting product is possible because, "with our superior knowledge of the community we serve we can continue to present community life and its problems in a more interesting manner." He expressed doubt that this suburban area offered a demand for a daily other than the Chicago metropolitans. "We feel that if such a need had existed, we [Paddock] would have started one."

The same point was raised in an editorial:

Are the suburbs ready to support new dailies, particularly within the home zone of four successful metropolitan dailies? If the new *Arlington Day* is successful, what will be the major distinguishing

---

[13] "Paddock Newspapers Tri-Weekly, March 1," *Editor & Publisher*, January 21, 1967.

[14] The material in this section is taken from *The American Press*, February, 1966.

differences between it and its metropolitan parents? Will the new *Arlington Day* carry substantial national advertising; will it be included as a major medium for Chicago's large mercantile retailers? . . . Will the weeklies' publishers seriously consider moving to blanket controlled circulation? If the *Day* is successful in attracting national advertising will the weeklies also participate? . . . In a sense the suburban press can interpret this Chicago development as a tremendous compliment. Clearly implied is (a) a suburban publishing potential greater than the advertising buyers have been willing thus far to admit and (b) the metropolitan press grows more aware of the difficulties of providing localized suburban coverage in central city media. Certainly every suburban publisher may be sure most metropolitan newspaper publishers are going to be watching this Chicago development closely.

Another indication that the *Arlington Day* was intended as a full-throttle test was the assignment of John Stanton, formerly a managing editor of the Chicago *Daily News,* as editor, and of Maurice Fischer, city editor of the *Daily News,* as managing editor. Stanton described his view of his mission: "The 44,000 residents of this dynamic and expanding community need a daily voice, and the businessmen of the area need a regular advertising medium. We aren't going to compete with the big metropolitan dailies; they do their job and do it well. But there is a great potential for a local daily, for the kind of lively 'here-at-home' newspaper we are going to put out. This will be an autonomous newspaper, not tied to 'downtown,' presenting a completely independent viewpoint."

The *Day* publications marked their first anniversary with frontpage editorials January 31, 1967, thanking readers and advertisers for making their first year a rewarding one. The editorials recalled the doubts expressed about the practicality of the venture, and said these doubts had been resolved by the fact that the two dailies at that point had a combined paid home delivery circulation in excess of 14,500, that most of the important food stores were now carrying ad schedules in the papers, and that projections for the next twelve months were for a doubling of advertising linage. "All of this," said the editorial in *Prospect Day,* "adds up to acceptance and approval far beyond our most optimistic hopes of a year ago. . . . We are looking forward to a great second year. Within a few weeks the *Day* will be printed at the new plant of our allied enterprise, The Metropolitan Printing Company in Elk Grove Village. It will be the most modern and versatile offset printing facility in the country; it will provide us with the finest color reproduction, high speed production, later deadlines and faster delivery."[15] These facilities would seem to indicate, too, that founding of other suburban publications by the company can be expected.

Another Model

Not to be left behind by its competition, the Chicago *Tribune* announced early in 1967 another model in the arsenal of weapons the metropolitan press has been bringing to bear on its suburban weekly competition. Area Publications Corporation was formed as a subsidiary of the Tribune Company to publish a tabloid-size newspaper called *The Trib* to be distributed Mondays, Wednesdays, and Fridays with the *Tribune*. The paper specializes in the local news of a selected group of western suburbs roughly in an area along the Chicago, Burlington & Quincy rail line from LaGrange to Naperville.

This approach obviously is designed to maintain circulation of the parent paper, since *The Trib* is added to the *Tribune* on three days a week, instead of being distributed as a separate, and possibly somewhat competitive paper. An offset printing plant in Hinsdale produces the paper.

To some extent this version supplements Neighborhood News sections which have been carried by the *Tribune* for a number of years, and if this pilot project is successful we may expect that additions will be made so that Neighborhood News sections will be entirely supplanted. Russell McFall, Neighborhood News editor who helped with the extensive research undertaken before the Tribune Company committed itself to this way of meeting the demand for local community news, in a conversation with the author, expressed the view that "suburban weeklies have reached their peak." He expects that experience will dictate many modifications and changes in this tri-weekly publication, and that the company will probably even try other formats and methods of distribution with publications in other suburbs, but that essentially the aim will

---

[15] Editorial, *Prospect Day*, January 31, 1967.

always be to strengthen the role and position of the parent *Tribune.*

In all of these efforts a primary consideration, of course, is to give the suburban reader a greater sense of identification with "his" newspaper. *The Trib* hopes to solidify this impression (and to a great extent carry it over to the *Tribune*) by re-plating front and back pages to make local editions for each of thirteen to fifteen communities to be served in the western area.

About the same time the Richmond (Va.) *Times-Dispatch* and its evening *News-Leader,* undertook a little different version, a weekly instead of a tri-weekly to be distributed at no extra charge with editions of the *Times-Dispatch* and *News-Leader* going into a predominantly rural area southwest of Richmond. The new weekly, called the *Southside Virginian,* is to have an independent editorial voice, and while its editorial offices are in Petersburg, production is out of the dailies' plant.

The "Piggy-back" Approach. One other competitive method with which some big dailies have experimented deserves at least brief mention, even though it is clear that it would always be limited to highly specialized situations. A note in the *NEA* (National Editorial Association) *Newsletter* for June, 1960, reported that "Suburban weeklies and dailies are teaming up with metropolitan papers in two cities to give the big papers added suburban coverage. The *Town News,* a weekly just turned daily in Pompano Beach, Florida, has arranged to be sold as the front section of the Miami Herald six days a week at the Herald's regular price. Same time, the Baltimore *Evening Sun* has begun to distribute a weekly inside the Wednesday edition of the regular daily to boost its suburban circulation."

Al Neuharth, former assistant executive editor with the Detroit *Free Press* and then general manager of the Rochester (N.Y.) *Times-Union* and *Democrat & Chronicle,* urged more experiments of this kind when he spoke to a 1964 meeting of the Associated Press Managing Editors Association at Phoenix. He recalled that the Florida combination had been preceded by a "piggy-back" arrangement between the Albany (N.Y.) *Knick-erbocker News* and the Saratoga Springs (N.Y.) *Saratogian* in the late 1950's, when both papers were members of the Gannett group. As *Editor & Publisher* reported Mr. Neuharth's proposal:

The two-in-one newspaper package Mr. Neuharth envisions will be made up of a true community newspaper, completely local in news and advertising, and with its own identity—coupled with a "true metropolitan paper, completely global in news and general in advertising. I see them delivered through one sales and service circulation organization, side by side if they are on the same publishing cycle. And where this is done, the result should be continued substantial circulation gains for the metro paper in the two-in-one package. . . . From a circulation standpoint suburban readers must be offered the two-in-one package at a somewhat reduced subscription price over what the two separate deliveries cost. The products must be so distinctive and the price so attractive that the vast majority of suburbanities will want to read both. . . ." In many areas the present trend towards zoned metro papers may continue a while longer. But many, if not most, of our big city publishers are ready and anxious for a way to get out from under expensive juggling acts with zoned editions. And many, if not most community dailies, would welcome ways to escape some of the costly complexities of trying to compete with their big city brothers.[16]

This author suggested in 1956 to a metropolitan daily an essentially similar plan, not for a suburban paper but for a community paper 300 miles from the metropolitan's point of publication. It was proposed as a method by which the big city morning paper, circulated statewide, could increase its circulation in areas dominated by other dailies. The community weekly would convert to a morning daily, be printed in the same early morning hours that the first edition of the big daily was being transported the 300 miles, and then be combined in a two-in-one package. It was expected that local news and advertising in the small community would not fill more than eight pages, sometimes only four, but on a five-day basis this would still be the equivalent of a 32–40-page weekly paper. Not more than a half-dozen situations throughout the area appeared to lend themselves well to such a procedure without raising a storm of protest from dailies whose territories would be infringed, and even in the favorable situations there were considerations of this sort. As a result it has never been tried, but some modification of this sort of package may indeed lie in the future as a result of the great advances in technology.

---

[16] "Predicts Two-in-One Newspaper Package," *Editor & Publisher,* December 12, 1964.

A Circulation Dilemma

Several references in this chapter to "shoppers" and to "controlled circulation newspapers" make desirable at this point some attempt at definitions.

Shoppers—As the name implies, these publications are directed at the potential customer of retail businesses, principally the housewife planning her grocery shopping. The advertiser is interested in reaching every potential customer in the area from which his store normally draws trade, hence he wants mass or saturation circulation. To give him that, the publisher distributes the publication free of charge to the home. Advertisers can get forms of mass coverage from other media, of course, but the shopping publication's ample space for detailed price listings which the customer can copy down on a list, compare with other quoted prices, or refer to hours or days after a first reading make the shopper a popular advertising medium. Others besides retailers are interested in the readership this detailed price advertising supposedly attracts—financial institutions, services, trades, and both contract and transient want ad users. The shopping publication may or may not carry any news; in any case the news and feature will be decidedly the minor part of the content. The shopper will not qualify as a newspaper under provisions of the laws of virtually all the states defining "legal newspapers" and these publications do not qualify for admission to the second-class mail privilege of the U.S. Post Office because of the lack of paid circulation.

Controlled Circulation—Some publications, in order to obtain mass circulation or to saturate an area to the satisfaction of advertisers, distribute the publication to every home in the area on a "voluntary paid" basis. That is, the carrier makes periodic calls on the householder to collect the stated charge for the publication. Whether the householder pays or not, he will continue to receive the publication regularly; if he fails to pay, or even refuses in order to have delivery discontinued, he will get the paper anyway but no further effort is made (for that period) to collect. All those who pay may then be listed as paid subscribers, and paid circulation is interpreted by advertisers as meaning that the householder values the publication, wants it continued, and therefore presumably reads it with some attention. That kind of proof is not available with the "shopper"; the advertiser can prove for himself if he wishes that the publication was delivered, but he does not know if it was read or immediately tossed in the trash. Whereas the shopper's distribution, whether by mail or by carrier, is wholly an item of expense, the controlled circulation newspaper has some hope of offsetting part or all of that expense through circulation revenue.

The Legal Newspaper—Legal in the sense that it meets a statutory definition, the paper offers its advertisers a wholly paid circulation—ostensibly, at least. The Post Office annually requires a sworn statement of circulation which is accepted as generally reliable, although Post Office officials have made little visible effort to check publishers' figures. The Audit Bureau of Circulations (ABC) serves weekly newspapers too, but the number of weeklies belonging to ABC has always been under 10 per cent of the total. The advertisers' interest in audited figures is reflected in the establishment of in 1963 a Certified Audited Circulations (CAC), a nonprofit corporation to serve controlled circulation and free distribution papers. It is similar to the ABC in that its board of directors is composed of representatives of advertisers, advertising agencies, and publishers, with the last-named in the minority.

Requirements for membership include publication for a minimum of six months; printing in an acceptable newspaper format; and the maintenance of printing, circulation, and delivery records in a manner which will facilitate auditing. Membership dues are based on circulation; auditing charges are extra. An auditor checks the member's records twice a year (once in two years for weeklies), and once during the year, without prior notice to the publisher, makes calls on a random sample of the households in the publication's circulation area.

Several years ago the Michigan Press Association bulletin to members said that at that time (1963) a number of publishers were considering switching from a fully paid basis to controlled or free circulation. . . . When the cost of maintaining circulation nearly equals the income it produces, there are publishers who feel they should adopt a controlled system and spend the effort previously devoted to circulation on more productive activities. Apparently these publishers were mostly in suburban areas where a rapid increase in population requires a constant, intensive effort to sell subscriptions. The standard approach, however, is to maintain the newspaper in its usual fully paid circulation status, and to give the advertiser his desired saturation coverage through an adjunct shopper. If his plant is efficient, the second publication usually returns to the publisher a handsome profit rather than being an extra burden. Some more conservative publishers find themselves pushed into starting the shopper when a huge new shopping center springs up in the community. The center management then proposes a shopper, and if the publisher is unwilling or unable to begin one, the management starts one. This happens, too, in communities where there is no local newspaper; there have been cases where a publication started solely as a shopping center advertising publication developed into a true community newspaper.

Which Way To Go? The running debate over whether or not the best course for weekly publishers is to turn to some form of controlled circulation has a long history. Opposing points of view were nicely summed up in an exchange of letters between two broadly experienced and knowledgeable publishers printed in *Editor & Publisher* in 1965. The argument was kicked off when one correspondent observed that in his experience an opposition shopper could succeed only in a community where the weekly is weak. Victor C. Leiker, publisher of the Middletown (N.J.) *Courier* and other papers, responded:

For years now I have printed suburban newspapers from a three-state area around metropolitan New York in addition to having edited and published several of my own ranging from county seat to the latest which is in a typical post-war suburban community. The weekly newspapers are in trouble and it isn't their fault either. There have been many poor weeklies that went under and I have seen some very fine and outstanding ones sold too. Mr. Wallace observes that "the shopper succeeds in the community because the weekly is weak." There may be exceptions where this applies but that is not anywhere near the truth. I can show him and anyone else who thinks this way some splendid weeklies that couldn't make it because of the competition from shoppers. I can show him many instances, too, where a shopper was needed and a weekly newspaper was not.

In many new communities large enough to support a healthy weekly the interest by the residents is so minor that circulation is an impossible situation. (This also applies to many prize-winning and outstanding small dailies.) People who move into these new communities "don't care" and they will be the first to tell you so. Regardless of the excellence of the local paper they have no interest in where they live; they will not subscribe and a shopper becomes a natural. In other cases the advertisers are not interested in the finest weekly or even the finest small town daily. They want mass circulation, 100 percent coverage, and they couldn't care less how the product looks. (I know what I'm talking about. I publish several of these money makers while our prize-winning weekly grubs along barely making ends meet.) . . . There are many good weeklies going under because the need of their existence is in question, not their quality.[17]

Robert Juran, managing editor of the Riverdale (N.Y.) *Suburban Trends,* then offered a point of view more to be expected of one clearly oriented to the editorial side, in contrast to the view of a publisher who might be incidentally an editor:

Mr. Leiker first of all says "weekly newspapers are in trouble." I challenge this statement. First of all, weekly circulation is at an all-time high. Next, many weeklies are increasing their frequency of circulation, and I'm sure all of us know of weeklies which have gone daily. This is trouble? If so, we all need more trouble. Mr. Leiker seems to feel many good weeklies are in hot water because of shopper competition. I would like him to give us some documentation of this. I believe a thorough study will show that in nearly all cases when a really good weekly is challenged by a shopper, the shopper loses out. . . . Mr. Leiker goes on to talk of advertisers who are "not interested in the finest weekly." They want mass circulation, he says. Well, the advertiser who wants mass circulation, as we all know, does not get anything resembling mass readership, and when he has spent his dollars on the shopper he winds up, in most cases, with less actual readership than if he bought the paid-circulation weekly. . . . If Mr. Leiker—who publishes both shoppers and newspapers—is, as he says, getting rich selling space in the shoppers, he is clearly a businessman who just happens to be in the newspaper business, not a newspaperman first and foremost. He is obviously plugging mass circulation and isn't selling his newspaper—the legitimate one—hard enough. . . . We here at *Trends* have proof of this, for when we were a 31,000 shopper our ad linage wasn't nearly as big as it is now that we have converted to ABC paid (more than 17,000). Either our merchants are getting a different sales pitch than Mr. Leiker's, or Mr. Leiker's newspaper (not shopper) doesn't provide the reader with the depth of coverage the merchants want. I'm talking about news coverage now. . . . When a weekly newspaper goes under, almost invariably it is because the town is

---

[17] "Letters to the Editor," *Editor & Publisher,* August 14, 1965.

dying or the management was apathetic and lazy, or both. Given a fight between a newspaper and a shopper, I'll put my money on the newspaper every time.[18]

It may be said that up to now, at least, instead of a trend to convert weekly newspapers into controlled circulation papers or free distribution shoppers, the movement has been almost all the other way. New newspapers started (principally in the suburbs) have usually circulated their first issues free, then gone to some form or other of controlled circulation, and as soon as feasible put the paper on a fully paid basis. The reasoning is easy to follow—free distribution is the quickest and easiest way to acquaint new customers with the product, advertisers will use space and pay a full rate from the very outset because of saturation coverage, and the paper thereby derives an income which at least comes close to meeting expenses. The incentive to go to paid circulation is of course to gain legal status as a newspaper, win second-class postal privileges, and to become a vehicle for public notice advertising. Beyond this seems to be the inherent desire of anyone who works with a newspaper format to make the product more and more like a genuine newspaper with fresh news, with local features, with editorial comment. The desire to have a "voice" may be subordinated for quite a while under a desire to make a business go, to make money, but eventually it comes out, and, as we shall note later, it emerges in many ways and takes many forms.

Still in Testing Stage

The "Third Force" has by no means settled into a format, agreed on a role, or found one broad path to follow to success. Some editors are convinced that the suburban paper should resemble a rural weekly in an urban center, with a "folksy, highly personal approach." They say they should offer "scrapbook newspapers," print the kind of news people have been accustomed to clip and save—birth notices, school achievements, weddings, anniversaries, obituaries. Other are equally convinced that ultimately suburban weeklies will fall into a pattern most

---

[18] "Orlando Sentinel and Star Join Chicago Tribune Family," *Editor & Publisher*, September 4, 1965.

nearly resembling news magazines—reporting the numerous and difficult social and economic problems of growing communities in depth, with a knowledgeable and sophisticated approach which requires well-educated and able staffers. They would minimize what they call "trivia" and which the other class of editors believe is the real news of interest to readers. The agreement is no more general in the area of editorial comment, yet this is the one role which the metropolitan dailies are wholly surrendering to the weeklies and evidently expecting them to perform. Hayden Reece, Suburban Sections editor for the Los Angeles *Times*, in describing how the five suburban sections published each week by the *Times* operate, says, "Local controversies are an area in which we tread carefully. Every effort is made to treat them with complete objectivity and the allotment of equal space to both sides in an issue. We leave all opinion and subjective comment *exclusively to the editor of the community paper*" (italics added).[19]

This self-awareness yet lack of agreement on what is considered to be "the unique function, responsibilities and challenges of the suburban press" led to formation on August 1, 1960, of the Suburban Press Foundation. Eight publishers in the Chicago area were the founding members, but by June, 1961, the Foundation had become national in scope (even international, with one Canadian member) and as of 1967 had a roster of 52 publishers printing about 200 newspapers in the major metropolitan areas. These could accurately be said to be the leaders in the suburban field.

The Foundation lists its aims as helping members to improve their overall performance through establishing and clarifying standards and practices, working in cooperation to develop circulation and promotion methods and to attract advertising linage, to cultivate professional growth in suburban journalism and to stimulate editorial leadership. The Foundation has held twice-a-year seminars for publishers, editors, and staff members, has reached an agreement with the journalism department of Northern Illinois University for an editorial critique service and a research program, has made some surveys of its own, and has coordinated efforts of members to develop career materials for high school and college journalism students and

[19] "Thirteen Years and Five Suburban Sections Later," *ASNE Bulletin*, April 1, 1965.

publication staff members. Each Foundation member publisher has equal status and responsibility in the group, whatever
the size of his newspaper operation.

Chester K. Hayes, who had made a vivid impression on the
Cook County Suburban Publishers Association when he spoke
at the group's annual meeting in 1959, was later invited to
serve as the first executive director of the new Foundation. His
experience with community newspaper problems dates back to
the 1920's, when he was on the staff of the Western Newspaper
Union, the principal supplier of readyprint and of syndicated
features designed especially for the weekly newspaper. Later he
organized and headed Business Consumer Communications, a
firm supplying a mat service to newspapers. One of the infant
Foundation's first steps was to appoint Dr. Curtis D. MacDougall, professor of journalism at Northwestern University and
author of textbooks on reporting and newsroom problems, as
editorial consultant. Dr. Granville Price of Northern Illinois
University filled that role following MacDougall.

Standards of membership exclude metropolitan neighborhood weeklies or semi-weeklies, although some publishers who
operate both neighborhood and true suburban papers are
eligible to hold membership for their suburban units. A newspaper has to have been established for at least two years before
it is eligible and show a record of financial stability and editorial responsibility satisfactory to the membership committee.

Since the Foundation declines the role of trade association
and says it is pursuing "a cooperative research, promotion, and
self-development program . . . not duplicated through membership in other trade and press associations" sporadic efforts
have continued to form a distinctive alliance or group which
would concentrate the suburbans' circulation strength for effective advertising representation on a national scale. One such
effort was made in August of 1966 when representatives of four
national groups, including the Foundation, met in Chicago with
Michael S. Lerner, business manager of the Lincoln-Belmont
Publishing Company of Chicago as chairman. Represented in
addition to the Foundation were the National Newspaper Association, the National Association of Advertising Publishers, and
the Accredited Home Newspapers of America. It was suggested
that the associations cooperate in establishing a sort of super-
board which could speak for the community newspaper in lob-

bying, circulation and advertising regulation, research, recruitment, and national or regional advertising sales. The proposal was referred to each of the four associations for further study.

In view of the general pattern of American life favoring inevitable "big business, big labor, big government," it may be assumed that efforts to build up the muscle of the community newspaper as an identifiable industry will continue, whatever form they may ultimately take. The approach illustrated by the meeting of representatives of the four associations is fraught with difficulties because of vested interests, conflicting philosophies, and the often-stressed individuality of the newspaper publisher. When the rewards of merger are made tangible enough, and put within reach, action follows. It awaits the emergence of a charismatic figure such as we have seen in the past inspiring and leading the huge combinations in big business and big labor.

And yet because of the distinctive role of the newspaper as a private enterprise which is also a quasi-public institution, there is no pattern of the past to follow for a combination to achieve "big" status. All efforts will be watched with apprehension on all sides and for that reason progress will be slow and halting. Yet the basic yearning for muscular development to exercise power will remain, and so the next several decades should be, as Damon Runyon used to say, an interval very interesting to watch indeed.

Chapter 6

PERCEPTION OF THE WEEKLY'S ROLE

SHERWOOD ANDERSON, at the height of his success as an author, became the publisher of two weekly newspapers in 1928, and reaffirmed something disgruntled editors had been saying in one way or another since the invention of movable type, "I think almost every man in the country has the belief, buried away in him somewhere, that he would make a successful newspaper editor." He speculated further that "almost every newspaperman has in him something of a writer. . . . There is the tremendous advantage of being in close and constant touch with every phase of life in an American community every day of the year. What could any writer ask more enticing than that?"[1]

The historical background reviewed herein, the record of proliferation of newspapers under most unlikely circumstances and their persistence under conditions of hardship, is not only testimony for the soundness of Anderson's belief but offers convincing evidence that some form of the community weekly newspaper will survive (and thrive) into the twenty-first century and beyond.

Never has there been any agreement on a formula for success in the community newspaper field beyond broad generalizations about the basic importance of news in the newspaper. "Only the misinformed hold to the idea that publishing a newspaper is an easy way to get rich," says Ben Blackstock, manager

---

[1] *Nearer the Grass Roots (and a Journey to Elizabethton)* (San Francisco: Westgate Press, 1929).

86

of the Oklahoma Press Association. "Making a profit on either a daily or weekly newspaper is a demanding task in the many skills it requires. . . . A newspaper almost defies classification as an enterprise. It involves manufacturing . . . good business management . . . something of a public utility . . . the whole complex of machines and the actual printing."[2]

Looking for a Formula?

To say there never has been a formula is not to say, however, that none has been offered. Editors themselves are fond of telling each other how to go about putting out better, more successful papers, and they appear to be equally willing to listen, at conventions of all kinds, as persons from allied fields—advertising men, magazine editors, typographical experts, journalism professors—tell them what their newspapers ought to be like and what steps they should take to achieve that perfection. When they ponder their future they turn for reassurance to a list of "functions of the community newspaper" offered by one of their elder statesmen, Houstoun Waring, who prior to his retirement in 1966 as editor of the Littleton (Colo.) *Independent* was perhaps the best known and most articulate weekly editor. His comments therefore were widely reprinted in the trade press, and can be used here as a springboard for further discussion:

    1. First of all, the newspaper makes a community's economy work by advertising. Cities' retail trade drops markedly when newspapers cease to operate even temporarily.
    2. The press permits the expression of public opinion through "Letters to the Editor" and by means of interviews. Thus, all sides of a question can be debated.
    3. The press has a decision-forcing function. Everyone may be aware that a community has drifted into a bad situation, for example. Massive publicity requires each citizen to take a stand; the evil can no longer be ignored because it is a topic of conversation.
    4. Newspapers have a status-conferring function. Anyone picked for mention is recognized as standing out from the crowd. Unfortunately, some newspapers confer status on underworld characters by glamorizing their daring or "gentlemanly" qualities.

---

[2] "Challenge of the Weekly Newspaper," *Oklahoma Publisher*, March, 1964.

5. Perhaps the most important function is that of acquainting community leaders with the activities of other leaders. The school directors learn through the paper what the state highway department is thinking. The ministers discover the problems of the County Welfare director. An organization planning a community event avoids a conflict of dates by press notification to other groups.

6. The newspaper helps the reader understand his environment. He learns when to pay his taxes, where to register his child in school, how to get a driver's license, whom to see for free polio shots, and what streams have been stocked with trout.

7. If the environment needs changes, the newspaper can assist citizens in crusading for improvement.

8. The press is a sounding board for policy. Public officials often send up "trial balloons" to determine the public reaction to a proposal.

9. The press strengthens moral resolution, especially in small cities where citizens don't live anonymously. Because tempted men fear newspaper publicity (just as they do an audit), they are better able to resist temptation. The press in a small and medium-sized city thus becomes, perhaps unwittingly, a community chaperon.

10. The press is a medium of entertainment, featuring hobbies, etc. Its comic strips have become America's folklore.

11. The press, by devoting so much space to sports, is what William James termed "a moral substitute for war." Americans for fifty years have thought more about basketball, golf, and horse racing than they have about the glories of Bull Run and Gettysburg. Readers vicariously identify themselves with a halfback rather than a major general.

12. The press attends to small wants. Through the classifieds it brings people together to solve their lost-found, rental, employment, and other problems.

13. Finally, the suburban press has a function that applies to America's 50 million suburbanites. This is to give them a sense of identity. All of us wish to belong to a definite community that has a spirit of its own.

Waring's list offers a considerably more pragmatic view than the hyperbole with which many editors have described their exalted role. Not at all atypical is the passage is an interesting old book compiled by John W. Moore of Concord, New Hampshire, in 1886. In describing the rapid spread of the community press in the first eighty years of the nineteenth century, Moore wrote lyrically:

We who are now living, some of us, have seen them [newspapers] change from mere vehicles of intelligence to engines of immense power, closely connected with the peace and prosperity of the people and the nation. . . . Well conducted newspapers have a tendency to disseminate useful information upon all important subjects of every name and nature; to keep the public mind awake and active; to confirm and extend the love of freedom; to correct the mistakes of the ignorant and the impositions of the crafty; to tear off the mask from corruptions attempted by designing men; and finally, to promote the union of spirit and of action among the most distant members of an extended community. Newspapers, to do all that is now expected of them, must be conducted by men of talent, learning, and virtue, in order that they may continue to be public blessings. We may well rejoice in the constant increase and cheapness of these trusty teachers.[3]

It will be noted that these recommendations bear heavily on the community newspaper's responsibility to offer editorial opinions, to lead, to perform a "watchdog" function. Reference has been made previously to surveys which show that fewer than half of the total number of community weeklies ever run editorials, and of those that do run some form of editorial comment at least occasionally, an indeterminate number offer only clipped or syndicated editorials. The objection may be made that virtually all the "better" weeklies run editorials and they are the ones that count, anyway. The truth of this may be even harder to determine because of the difficulty of agreeing on criteria which will identify the "better" papers. If it is to be a matter of placing in general excellence categories in state and national contests, then editorial-less papers will never appear because the contest scoring tables always include a substantial number of points for editorial page. If a paper doesn't have one it isn't going to rank among the "better" papers, no matter how excellent it may be in other categories.

Why wouldn't a community newspaper offer editorial comment today? Reasons offered are many and various; here are typical comments:

"I don't have the information and background to comment intelligently on the complex issues of the day, either in the nation or my community." "No one on the staff has time to do the research and writing for editorials." "My primary function is to give the news, not to tell people what to think about it." "We lose too many subscribers, alienate too many advertisers with hard-hitting editorials; no other kind is any good." "I can tell my readers what's

---

[3] *Moore's Historical, Biographical, and Miscellaneous Gatherings Relative to Printers, Printing, Publishing and Editing* (Concord, N.H.: Republican Press Assn., 1886).

going on, can 'guide' them through interpretive, in-depth news articles." "I prefer to accomplish my objectives by working behind the scenes, reasoning with community leaders, rather than by stirring up resentment through editorials." "Too few readers actually read editorials to make them worth the effort, time, and space."

For some editors the excuse that they lack vision, writing skill, and background needed to produce good editorials is undoubtedly true. It has always been true of a good share of publishers and editors; it was common practice all through the 1800's for lawyers, teachers, physicians, and other professional men with superior educations to write the editorials for the papers in their communities. In the heyday of the political party press the political leaders provided the pungent comment, usually unsigned and therefore attributable to the printer who was nominally the editor and publisher. To be sure, this was not universally the case; one of the strong impulses that drives a man to establish or buy a weekly newspaper is the desire to be heard, to make his opinions known on a broader scale than in conversations or from a more effective forum than a soapbox. This primary incentive may later be eroded by pressures of time, of making the business go, of "getting along."

For "The Real Opinion"

In larger weekly newspaper enterprises, that is, anything capable of supporting at least a couple of front-office employees, it should not matter if the owner and publisher believes himself to be incapable of writing editorials. His hired editor can be assigned to the task, and if the publisher does not wish to give the employee full rein in expressing opinion, he can give the editorialist his opinions orally to be put into the words of the written editorial. For editorial expression in the small community, sincerity, frankness, honesty are qualities much to be valued above felicity of expression. It is doubtful if the old-time practice of getting others in the community to write the regular editorials would be effective now except in isolated cases. The readers would quickly come to regard these as they do the syndicated columnists in the metropolitan papers—readable, interesting, sometimes convincing, sometimes irritating, but not the "real opinion" of the newspaper. And it must be remembered that any newspaper, large or small, takes on an individuality, a personality of its own, separate from that of any of its writers. That seems to be why the often-suggested practice of signed editorials never catches on.

At any rate most of those, past or present, who comment on the weekly press brush aside the reasons for not running locally written editorials and emphasize the importance of the opinion function. Absence of editorial opinion is often a basic reason for maligning the shopper, although there is no reason why a shopper can't carry editorials, and some do. Professor Kenneth R. Byerly of the University of North Carolina, in an article discussing newspaper contest judging, titled "What Makes a Newspaper Great?" said there are "five major things . . . that make a weekly or daily newspaper outstanding," and in second position he placed strong editorial policy. (The other four, in order, are (1) news coverage, (3) money and business, (4) service, and (5) kindliness.) The last quality he further defined as "heart, or consideration for others," and of course both service and kindliness may be key ingredients of a strong editorial policy.[4]

The general acceptance of the weekly newspaper's opinion function is nowhere better demonstrated than in the outraged complaints of those who find evidence that the responsibility is being evaded, diluted, or misused. An outstanding example is the article in *Harper's* for December, 1964, written by a noted crusading reporter and press critic, Ben H. Bagdikian. He called the ideal of the community newspaper as the grass-roots opinion-maker "an unperishing myth" and said that with a few notable exceptions "most small dailies and weeklies are the backyard of the trade, repositories for any piece of journalistic junk tossed over the fence, run as often by print-shop proprietors as by editors." His target was the practice of some newspapers (far too many) of running as their own editorials propaganda mailed to them from special-interest sources—usually right wing, he added.

The criticism was not directed at material which is openly attributed, although good journalists decry puffery in either news or editorial columns (if for no other reason that that it's poor business), but at the material sent by syndicates or editorial services in which the true source is concealed or carefully minimized. Bagdikian chose one firm, which he said is not the

---

[4] "What Makes a Newspaper Great?" *Editor's Forum* (Atlanta: Georgia Press Assn., August, 1965).

largest, to illustrate handling of the free canned editorial. These firms should not be confused with syndicates which provide editorials as one of a group of feature services for which the newspaper pays a fee. There is no great objection to a service of this kind other than that the editorials provided necessarily must be highly general, bland, suitable for the varying tastes of a number of clients in different sections. No, the objection is to the editorial service which provides a packet of editorials each week to the newspaper free of charge; the firm meets its expenses and presumably makes a profit by charging another firm or an association a fee to put its point of view or a hidden commercial pitch in the editorials. The firm used as an example in the article was said to have a mailing list of 1,199 weeklies and 150 dailies, and Bagdikian said that a typical editorial will be "picked up by about two hundred papers, each one run as the local paper's own opinion, usually on its editorial page." The result, Bagdikian charged, is that "almost any private citizen or special group can buy his way into the editorial columns of smaller papers with relative ease and low cost."[5]

Role of Rationalization

The author, in his experience as a weekly newspaper editor, was familiar with a Pacific Coast firm which each week mailed a packet of editorials. Close reading of the material would easily reveal the clients, who were of such types as electric light and power company groups, grocers' alliances, the American Medical Association, fruit packers' associations, Association of Western Railroads, etc. The pieces were skillfully written, the source was usually indicated in the body of a piece, but in a casual, offhand way, the point of view was presented in a balanced, rational way, often backed with impressive statistics. The truly insidious part was the way in which the editor could so readily believe the editorial crystallized his own point of view, and he thereupon rationalized the use of the piece in his editorial columns, ostensibly as one of his own editorials, because "it represents what I think, said in a manner better than I could say it." As a salve to the conscience some editors might

[5] "Behold the Grass-Roots Press, Alas!" *Harper's,* December, 1964.

credit it to the syndicate, just as they might use a credit line for an editorial picked up from a neighboring newspaper and submitted to the reader as representing an interesting point of view from another community. Bagdikian agreed that most editors who ran such editorials did so because they agreed with the point of view, and perhaps would say roughly the same things if they wrote the editorials themselves. "But there is a profound difference," he insisted, "between the identical National Association of Manufacturers editorial appearing in six hundred newspapers and six hundred editors thinking and writing about what the NAM has to say." Then he came to the point which epitomizes the outrage felt by critics of what they feel is an abuse of the editorial responsibility:

Because rural papers have a disproportionate political impact and because they happen to be the major carriers of canned opinion, we are confronted with a perverse rule: *The smaller the newspaper, the greater its relative influence in national politics* [his italics].[6]

Similar outrage was expressed by Robert U. Brown, editor of *Editor & Publisher,* with a similar (implied at least) tribute to the supposed editorial power and effectiveness of the weekly press. Brown was objecting to what he called a "barrage of editorials" sent out by National News-Research of Washington, D.C., urging opposition to repeal of Section 14(b) of the Taft-Hartley Act. He examined the rationalization an editor might use that "regardless of authorship, regardless of the source, if these words express a point of view that coincides with mine and say it better than I could say it when I see nothing wrong with embracing them as my own," and rejected it as naïve:

This isn't fair to the reader who credits the editor with undeserved authorship and erudition. It doesn't take into account, either, the persuasiveness of the original author who may convince an editor unable to make up his mind that "this is the way I really feel about it." And it doesn't credit the design and motives of the authors and distributors who do so for a price.[7]

Brown mentioned a proposal by Representative Frank Thompson, Jr., of New Jersey for a law to require canned edi-

---

[6] *Ibid.*
[7] "Shop Talk at Thirty," *Editor & Publisher,* April 23, 1966.

torials to be labeled as such, identifying those who bought and paid for the editorial space. Brown said such a law probably would be unconstitutional but "one other way to eliminate them is for every state publishers' and press association to take a public stand on the issue. A grass roots condemnation of the practice would have a lot of influence on editors, even the smallest ones who may not belong to the association. What we need are editors who have the guts to admit on their editorial pages either that 'I have nothing to say on this subject today,' or 'I haven't had time to write anything for this space this week,' and leave it blank. Or, if they fill the space with material from other sources, that they label it properly as to its source for the edification of their readers."

Editors Little Concerned

In thirty-five years of attending state press association meetings, and reading about many others, the author noted very, very few references to canned editorials, and those were always just suggestions to dispense with them because locally written copy would be so much more effective, even if the editor's style was admittedly inept. (Long before Bagdikian's article, the author used as an interesting class exercise a little competition in which students were asked to try to identify editorials in weekly papers which had been provided by the Pacific Coast firm mentioned earlier. Usually the students could spot them. That provided a take-off point for the lecture on propagandists' efforts to use both the news and editorial columns of the community press.)

Shouldn't the editor be a more jealous guardian of the power and leadership responsibility the foregoing criticisms attribute to him? The trouble seems to be that many editors do not agree that they have any such influence (a position which must be held by those who do not run editorials at all) and that many assessments by scholarly observers tend to downgrade the influence of the community newspaper editor and publisher. These studies take the position that changing conditions of American life, the multiplication of educational agencies and of media of mass communication have greatly lessened the dependence of readers on the weekly press for either information or guidance and advice. Few would agree, though, with the late Lucius Beebe's reading of journalistic history, denying that true influence ever existed. In his account of the storied *Territorial Enterprise* in Nevada he wrote:

The pretensions to holy endeavor and elevated moral tone which came to American journalism later and which are possessed of all the plausibility of an opera hat on a Pawnee were unknown to an earlier generation of practitioners. Editors made no claims as guardians of public morals and seldom boasted of their wakeful vigilance of heart as preceptors of universal virtue. The right-thinking, forward-looking and professional ethics to which modern publishers lay claim would have reduced Joe Goodman or Dennis McCarthy [early-day publishers of the *Enterprise*] to inextinguishable laughter. American journalism was then as it has always been, a hilarious and disreputable calling which fetched the fancy of uninhibited practitioners of chicane and fraudulence. But it never, as is the fashion of a fraudulent age, assumed the mantle of prophetic dignity which was imagined by the Pulitzers, Reids, and Ochses of a later generation. No schools of journalism existed to elevate the spurious to the exalted level of fictitious respectability.[8]

Beebe's competence as a historian may be assumed to be limited to railroads, and whatever pertinence his assessment of early day journalism may have must be limited to the mining-boom days of Nevada. Unquestionably many of the land-boom papers, those printed to run homestead notices, and those founded to serve special advertising functions, made no pretense of offering meaningful editorial comment. On the other hand, the volume of testimony is overwhelming that early day editors did regard editorial comment as the principal part of their mission; hence the vast number of political party papers. We have noted that concern with local news was a comparatively late development for small papers out in the hinterlands.

One effort to determine how weekly newspaper editors and publishers evaluated their own power found small community journalists rather vague and inconclusive about their role and effectiveness. Robert M. Shaw and Lee Irwin, while on the journalism faculty at the University of Washington, conducted in-depth interviews at 117 weekly newspapers in the state of Washington and then issued a series of reports based on their findings concerning aspects of weekly newspaper editorial and

---

[8] *Comstock Commotion: The Story of the Territorial Enterprise* (Palo Alto: Stanford University Press, 1954).

business operations. The authors stated four major conclusions:

(1) About half of the publishers interviewed do not consider the main function of their newspaper to transmit factual information, but to promote and develop "community consciousness"—that is, community harmony.

(2) Publishers try to "get things done" in their communities by the use of two main methods: first, the use of publicity of facts or comments to bring public opinion to bear on an issue; and second, the use of their personal influence in cooperation with influential persons in the community. The combinations of these two methods are extremely complex.

(3) Publishers who work closely with the "power structure" of influential persons in the community seem to be more effective in "getting things done" than those who consider their function to be purely a journalistic one.

(4) In the light of these three conclusions, it naturally follows that the use of a publisher's power purely by journalistic means is only half effective. The main policy decisions in a small community are rarely made in free, frank and open discussion, but through a complex network of personal relationships. Therefore, the publisher who consciously limits his function to printing the facts and commenting on them is not making intelligent use of his total effectiveness.[9]

Readers Ambivalent

Weekly newspaper editors have been telling each other for a century or more in conventions and in trade publications that the editorial page is the "heart and soul" of the newspaper; that a newspaper which fails to carry editorial comment or otherwise try to exert leadership in a community is abdicating its responsibility. How do the readers feel? Do they agree?

Such limited evidence as there is points strongly to a kind of ambivalence among readers. They will deny that *they* are persuaded or convinced by editorial stands taken by the newspapers they read, yet if they are in opposition to such policies they may strongly decry the effect on *others,* complain about a monopoly of the press in their community, accuse the press of unfairly swaying voters or of failing to do what it should on particular public issues.

---

[9] *Publishers' Power,* Report No. 6 in a survey of Washington weeklies, June, 1960.

A study reported in *Journalism Quarterly* first tried to identify a commonly accepted group of community leaders (the community power structure) and then asked them what they believed the newspaper's leadership role should be. Only one leader in a group of forty-six said that it should be the newspaper's role to *initiate* community projects. Thirty-nine per cent of the respondents would confine the newspaper's role in community projects to providing publicity (reporting the "facts" in news stories) but 59 per cent said the proper role would be to "work jointly with community leaders to initiate projects." The most frequent response was that the newspaper should reflect the ideas of the whole community in a nonpartisan manner. Asked about projects which are controversial, the panelists most frequently responded that the newspaper should just "present the facts" or "give both sides." About a third said that the weekly newspaper should take the initiative in publicizing controversy, but 10 per cent said the paper should play down or exclude controversies, and 53 per cent said the paper should publicize controversies only when others have discussed them. The authors summarized their findings by saying, "While they [the community leaders] were willing to accept some degree of *participation*, they actually preferred the *publicity* function."[10]

One making a casual survey of the rapidly growing field of literature dealing with "the community power structure" will be struck by the paucity of references to the power or influence of weekly newspapers and their editors and publishers. Where newspapermen are mentioned, their *economic* role is likely to be seen as the relevant factor in their leadership status—they will be said to have influence because they rank among the leading *businessmen*, active in the Chamber of Commerce, the Rotary Club, the country club. Most of the case studies use the "reputational" technique of identifying the supposed power structure; that is, by one means or another a sizeable panel is assembled of those whose opinions are believed to have some validity and who are supposed to have some knowledge of the "inner workings" of the community. From the panel's responses one or more small sets of "influentials" may be determined. In study after study these influentials, either by direct statement or by the inference which may be drawn from their failure to

---

[10] Alex S. Edelstein and J. Blaine Schulz, "The Weekly Newspaper's Role as Seen by Community Leaders," *Journalism Quarterly*, Autumn, 1963.

mention the media, disparage the role of all of the mass media of communication (not just the newspaper) both in their own thinking and on community projects in general. Leaders in a city of 22,000, where the daily was small enough to be considered a community newspaper not much different in nature from a large weekly, tended to believe that any project could succeed in their city even against the expressed opposition of the newspaper, and only one of twenty-eight respondents believed the newspaper's strong opposition could kill a project. This was despite a generally favorable image of the newspaper among these leaders, who agreed almost unanimously that the paper did support community-wide projects. About half of the leaders saw themselves as first planning the worthwhile projects for the town, then enlisting the editor's support.

Something of an exception to the general tendency of the students of "the community power structure" to ignore editors and their newspapers is found in a compilation which summed up the findings of eleven case studies. Here the authors came to a conclusion that:

It may be necessary to include in this kind of analysis the sector of mass communications that was omitted by Miller and Hunter [sociologists who have been in the forefront of community power studies; Hunter's "Community Power Structure" (1953) is considered a pioneering effort in this field]. Newspaper editors or owners were found among both the top and key influentials in four of the five southwestern U.S. cities studied. In the study of issues it appeared that understanding the local decision-making process may not be possible without giving adequate attention to the strategy position of the newspaper editor. Evidence from our present study demonstrates that major issues have been successfully resolved or blocked by the position taken by the newspaper editor. On the other hand, Miller's data suggest a relative absence of access by representatives of other communications media, such as radio and television.[11]

The authors speculate that an editor's tenure, or length of residence in the community, is a key factor in the amount of influence he may have and point to the fact that he does tend to get involved in just about every project, either because he himself may be among those who initiate it, or because the influentials come to him for publicity to support their proposals.

[11] W. V. D'Antonio et al., "Institutional and Occupational Representatives in Eleven Community Influence Systems," *American Sociological Review*, June, 1961.

As is to be expected, editors who are among the most prominent exponents of the newspaper's responsibility in community leadership are firmly convinced of the rightness of such policy. Eugene Cervi, the colorful editor-publisher of *Cervi's Rocky Mountain Journal* at Denver, told a Washington state newspaper convention in 1964, "fundamentally a good newspaper in the American tradition ought to regain the confidence of the public by performing courageously in social force and leadership in behalf of the lowest element of our society in order to insure that it is serving all of the people. This is not being done in the country today." He warned:

American dailies and entrenched noncompetitive weeklies as we know them today are hastening their own funeral through their inability to hold inward deterioration brought on by past excuses and abuses. . . . Their decline began in their greed to corner the power of knowledge and expression. The newspapers assumed an impossible assignment of covering and commenting on everything— and it must be said they did a remarkably able job, from their point of view, before the age of speed and new discernment. As . . . reduced competition came to more and more cities across the land, thus more easily insuring survival, the newspapers have become scorekeepers. . . . Some few consider themselves referees and umpires. But that isn't what the Constitution framers had in mind and that is not the vigilance that liberty requires. . . . It's in the neglected areas of humanistic studies, endeavors and purposes that far-reaching opportunities await the intelligent and sensitive editor who by the nature of things ought always to be the owner of his paper or at least the clearly unshackled captain of his course. An editor without the power of final decision isn't much of an editor— and an editor who has the power of decision and doesn't use it isn't much better.

The very extent of an editor's inevitable involvement, whether or not he consciously seeks it, subjects him to criticism even if he sticks to "reporting the facts" and does not carry a line of his own opinion in the paper. He is serving many constituencies and in each there will be some division, some antagonism. Ed Howe, the famous Kansas contemporary of William Allen White, said, "Newspapers are always unpopular, however good they are." In his book *Plain People* he recalled that he "once heard an editor say an honest newspaper is impossible, there is so much natural opposition to honest measures. I believe the most worthy and useful newspaper I ever knew had most bitter enemies, most of them among excellent citizens. . . . There is always demand for a campaign of abuse against an editor, particularly if he is successful. The great weakness of newspapers is that the people have too much voice in their management. . . ."[12]

Constituency of the Weekly

Critical observers of the press are likely to see deficiencies from the standpoint of the constituency in which they are especially interested, and to slight or ignore the problems created by demands from others in the distinguishable, and often disparate, audiences of a medium. This is quite vividly illustrated by a passage in John Lofton's *Justice and the Press* discussing the effect of public pressures on the machinery of justice: "The press, at its best, when guided by responsible owners and editors, can and does promote the cause of justice. At its worst, the press can do and does grave harm to the cause of justice. Yet even when it is doing an injury to justice, the press is not acting as a detached institution, independent of and unrelated to the society which it serves. Its words and outlook are dictated to a greater or lesser degree by that society. . . . Officials tend to react as their social backgrounds dictate and as their various constituencies demand. . . . But the press, too, has its constituency, which is similar to but not necessarily identical with that of the officers of the law."[13]

The community press indeed "has its constituency"; it has many. And they are diverse, yet mingled and shifting. The retail businessmen, the farmers, the unionized workers, the teachers and pupils in the high school, the members of women's clubs, the members of veterans' or fraternal organizations, the teen-agers, the senior citizens, the parents, the nonparents—the list could be stretched almost endlessly. And at a time when the problems of a single constituency seem most pressing to it—as for example when the persons involved in law enforcement in a community engage in a discussion of procedures to assure fair trial—the newspaper in the community may have attention focused on one narrow aspect of its operations and its responsibilities. Comments made about unsatisfactory performance

---

[12] *Plain People* (Binghamton, N.Y.: Vail-Ballou Press, 1929).
[13] *Justice and the Press* (Boston: Beacon Press, 1966).

in this one area will tend to imply that performance is equally unsatisfactory in all areas. The next constituency may repeat the process, and the next. The dissatisfied tend to be more emotional, hence more vocal, than the satisfied or the disinterested. The cumulative result may be more than a little discouraging for the editor conscientious about offering opinion on community affairs.

Yet the feeling is virtually unanimous, and has deep historical roots, that an attempt to offer leadership IS the proper role of the community newspaper; that a newspaper isn't truly a newspaper unless it makes the attempt. One of the first sociologists to attempt to analyze the weekly newspaper quantitatively, Dr. Malcolm M. Willey, recognized this in 1926: "Potentially the newspaper, especially the country weekly newspaper published in and for the small city and small town, can play an important part in developing the socialized community."[14]

The almost mystic view of the editor's role is epitomized by Walter Howey in his book *Fighting Editors*. He recalls the words of his first newspaper mentor who offered him the editorship of a country weekly: "A man must study for an editorship almost as long and hard as one would study for the priesthood. You are thinking only of the fascinating adventures in the newspaper business. Did you ever think about the responsibility of an editor to his readers? If you will take this job . . . it will give you a chance to realize the great value of becoming an advocate for the prosecution and for the defense. . . . No newspaper except a good newspaper can expect to live. A newspaper thrives on the appreciation of the public it serves."[15]

A widely held impression that publishers become more cautious as the value of their newspaper investment rises, and take fewer stands which might endanger that investment, is refuted by Phillip H. Stevens.[16] His data supported a conclusion that the greater the net income of a weekly newspaper, the more inclined its editor is to get involved in a local controversy. Responses from three-quarters of the 145 editors who replied

[14] "Community, Socialization, and the Country Newspaper: A Study in Newspaper Content," *Publications of the American Sociological Society,* 1926.

[15] *Fighting Editors* (Philadelphia: David McKay Co., 1946).

[16] "Controversy in the Weekly Press: A Study of Community Leadership" (Master's thesis, University of Wisconsin, 1961).

to his questionnaire indicated that "getting involved in a good local fight is a way of exercising community leadership." Something over 40 per cent of these editors had college or university training, but not all in journalism. This study correlates with the community power research which shows that influentials are generally those in the higher economic brackets.

The Newspaper as a Business

Nevertheless, it is when community newspapers move to protect some aspect of their *business* operations that they draw the heaviest public criticism. A good example of this occurred during World War II when Senator John H. Bankhead of Alabama submitted a bill to "authorize the Secretary of the Treasury to purchase and use advertising space in newspapers during each fiscal year for the duration of the war and 6 months thereafter in advertising the sale of bonds, notes, and other obligations of the United States, and for the publication in such newspapers as a part of such advertising, information, sales arguments, and appeals relating to and promoting or encouraging such sales." The Bankhead Act, providing for a maximum expenditure of 15 million dollars a year for such advertising in towns of 10,000 or less, passed the U.S. Senate at the end of 1943. The companion bill in the House, sponsored by Representative Cannon of Missouri, did not limit application to newspapers in cities under 10,000. Opponents of the bills argued that this would amount to a "subsidy" for the press, and a number of large metropolitan dailies strongly voiced disapproval of the bills. The Legislative Committee of the National Editorial Association scoffed at the subsidy charge, saying, "No advertiser controls the press and the government, as an advertiser, would be no exception. . . . Subsidy is merely silly talk with an ulterior motive behind it!"[17] The committee contended the government needed to advertise aspects of its war effort, and clearly implied that the opposition of the metropolitan dailies was based on resentment because they couldn't have the whole pie to themselves instead of sharing with small

[17] Letter to members of the NEA from Ed M. Anderson, NEA Legislative Committee chairman, August 31, 1943.

dailies and weeklies. The legislation failed in the House and the furor quickly died down.

Critics have been quick, too, to use the word "subsidy" in connection with the newspaper industry's long-running battle to maintain favorable second-class postage rates. Battles swirled around the free-in-county mailing provision until ultimately it was abolished. The then Postmaster General, Jesse Donaldson, testifying before a Congressional committee in 1949 in favor of general rate increases and drastic revision of second-class mail provisions, argued that, "What the publishers know—but what most folks do not know—is the present second-class rates are a survival of one of the early Congressional acts made under conditions that have long since ceased to exist. Very few people outside of the publishing business know of the free mailing privileges within the county of publication."[18] He added that in his opinion the publishing business was now largely a commercial undertaking and no more a public benefactor than the grocer, druggist, hotel or restaurant operator, or any other merchant rendering an essential public service. And here, too, there was a split between dailies and weeklies. The NEA said, "Post Office reports for 1944 to 1946 show that the dailies enjoy the chief benefits from free-in-county by a ratio of more than two-to-one over the weeklies."[19] The Postal Committee of the American Newspaper Publishers Association, said if there was a subsidy it wasn't for newspapers but for rural free delivery and other postal services improperly charged against second-class, and then added, "The greater the increase in second-class mail rates, the heavier the burden on the small newspapers and on people living in rural communities, small towns, and hamlets."[20]

These critics also took note of the consistent opposition on the part of organizations and publications representing the weekly newspaper to such legislation as bills to increase the minimum wage, or to bring certain white-collar workers (editorial and advertising employees) under minimum wage provisions; to the Wagner Act as "opening the door to professional organizers"; to certain aspects of social security, child labor and

[18] *NEA Legislative Bulletin,* July 16, 1949.
[19] *NEA Legislative Bulletin,* April 7, 1947.
[20] *Ibid.*

similar laws which many thought they should instead be vigorously supporting on behalf of their readers.

First Rule: Stay Alive

Still, the concern of publishers with the business side of their enterprise, however much they and others may regard it as quasi-public, should be perfectly understandable. The financially unsuccessful newspaper can't last. The evidence shows that a newspaper which is financially independent will also be more independent and more forceful editorially. Professor Byerly's list of qualities necessary to make a newspaper great, which is given on page 91, mentioned prominently the necessity of devoting attention to "money and business." The late Bill Long, manager of the Colorado Press Association, not long before his untimely death, compiled a list of ten points on "Hometown Newspaper Publishing for Fun and Profit." He listed the "for profit" points first: (1) Take care of your accounts and your accounts will take of you. (2) Run your business (the tough, hard decision-making; managing your own time). (3) Sell circulation. (4) Find new things to sell (office supplies, legal blanks, etc.). (5) If in doubt, take a raise (it's up to you to know what your rates should be, and raise them accordingly). And the five points "for fun": (1) Involve the family. (2) Draw your psychic dividends (the status your newspaper can give you in your community, area, and state). (3) Buy back some time each day. (4) Do one thing the best you can each issue. (5) Once each year look some important person in the eye—who needs it—and tell him to go to hell.

The finest opportunities for the last point lie in another area where the public apparently has simply conceded all the responsibility to the press (here the term can be interpreted broadly to cover all the mass media), that of defending the "public's right to know." The public's expectations are implicit in the statements to researchers—"give the facts; give both sides; the function is to *inform*." Yet the perverse reaction mentioned by Howe and others will frequently operate—in the small community a vigorous newspaper's sturdy attempts to get all the news will arouse resentment among a not inconsiderable portion of the audience; the publisher will have ample opportu-

Mark Lang

attainable from a technology view-point'' (Business Day, Sept. 15).

Apparently, Mr. Skinner is un-aware of European manufacturing technology. The AX-10, produced by Citroën, gets 76 miles a gallon, at a constant highway speed of 56 miles

In Virginia Beach, a Co

To the Editor:

"Apartheid at Virginia Beach'' (Op-Ed, Sept. 18) by Reginald A. Boddie, on Labor Day weekend, con-tains numerous inaccuracies. As Mayor of Virginia Beach, I want to set the record straight.

It surprised me that Mr. Boddie was unaware of the 1989 Labor Day riots in Virginia Beach. News media accounts of the $1.4 million in damage from riots and looting appeared na-

10-3-90

Prof. John C. Sim, 79, An Expert on the Press

John Cameron Sim, a professor emeritus at the University of Minnesota who was an authority on community press and scholastic journalism, died Sept. 25 at a nursing home in Minneapolis. He was 79 years old and lived in Minneapolis.

His family said he died of complications of diabetes.

A graduate of the University of Minnesota, Professor Sim joined the faculty at the Minnesota School of Journalism and Mass Communication in 1956, specializing in the community press and copy editing. He previously taught at the University of North Dakota and the University Alabama and for 10 years was editor and co-publisher of The East Grand Forks (Minn.) Record.

His book "Grass Roots Press: America's Weekly Newspapers," published in 1969, was ranked among the 200 leading journalism books by the American Association of Schools and Departments of Journalism. He also wrote a history of the Minnesota High School Press Association and a book-length report for Unesco, "Teaching About the Mass Media in Secondary Schools in the United States."

He is surivived by a daughter, Erin Sim of Minneapolis; a son, John of San Diego, and a sister, Dorothy Baker of Hemet, Calif.

nity to look a prominent citizen in the eye and tell him to go to hell. Usually the reason will be a request to suppress news, but it may be an official's attempt to close a meeting legally open to the public or to refuse access to a public record.

The annals are filled with shining examples of weekly newspapers' devotion and courage in defending the concept of "the right to know," but the uneasy feeling persists that the record is being compiled by a pitifully small fraction of all our newspapers.

Chapter 7

HOW IS THE COMMUNITY NEWSPAPER CHANGING?

THE AMERICAN RURAL WEEKLY is valueless, lily-livered and moribund." This devastating indictment would have been painful enough coming from any source, but because it came from a man labeled by *Time* magazine as publisher of "the U.S.'s largest and most prosperous country weekly," the Lapeer County (Mich.) *Press,* the debate it touched off in the trade press involved more soul-searching than the invective which might have been predicted from experiences of the past. *Time's* interview with Robert Marshall (Bob) Myers credited him with saying that the weekly press is run by printers who stuff their pages with syndicated hayseed features and eke out precarious livings on job-printing contracts. " 'The political power of the country weekly,' says Myers [said *Time*], 'is a grand illusion. More than half of the nation's 9,000 weeklies never print an editorial. Those that do are generally reactionary.' "[1]

Publishers' Auxiliary then printed an interview in which Myers qualified the sentiments attributed to him: "It's true of 75 per cent of the weeklies, but it still leaves more than 2,000 that are good newspapers. And for many of the 75 per cent there is a reasonable explanation."[2] In essence, the explanation was that a weekly in a 1,000-population town couldn't gross

[1] "Success in the Sticks," *Time,* December 21, 1962.
[2] "Editor Denies All Weeklies 'Lily-Livered,' " *Publishers' Auxiliary,* January 5, 1963.

enough revenue to justify very many employees and that "such a man is going to be 90 per cent printer and 10 per cent editor because he isn't going to have time to sit down at a typewriter and he can't afford to hire someone to do it for him."

An editorial in the *Publisher's Auxiliary* accused *Time* of slanted reporting for not mentioning Myers' qualification of his charges, and that drew a prompt retort from Editor Roy Alexander of *Time,* who said in a letter to the *Auxiliary,* "*Time*'s story obviously was not an evaluation of country weeklies by the editors, but a clearly labeled opinion of Mr. Myers. While we hold no brief for Mr. Myers' obviously bald pronouncement, we trust you will agree with us that, coupled with his outstanding success as publisher of the U.S.'s largest and most prosperous weekly, his comments are newsworthy. You may recall that *Time*'s editors did undertake a thorough-going assessment of the weekly press several years ago. If so, you will also remember that the *Auxiliary* and hundreds of weeklies across the country gave that very upbeat report on the characteristics and contributions of the hometown press banner headlines and quoted it liberally in promotion material for long afterward."[3]

'Twasn't the First Time

But that wasn't the first time that a forthright young editor had expressed a disillusioned view about the reactionary attitudes of so many of his colleagues—and had drawn equally sharp reaction. John C. Obert, a Nieman Fellow who was editor of the Alexandria (Minn.) *Park Region Echo,* wrote an article for the July, 1959, *Nieman Reports* titled "Whatever Happened to the Country Press?" which might have been the source of one of Myers' quotes. Obert said, "Far too many of the nation's 9,000 country editors share a grand illusion that they run the country." Later, in the debate occasioned by his article, he remarked, "I was not the first to make that assertion. I quoted several other sources substantiating the fact of this illusion."[4]

Obert's article was inspired by "a portrait of a typical editor" in the trade publication *The American Press,* based on the

[3] "Letters to the Editor," *Publishers' Auxiliary,* January 19, 1963.
[4] "Defends Harvard, Nieman Foundation and Himself Against Payton's Attack, *The American Press,* November, 1959.

results of twenty-five opinion polls conducted among weekly editors by the magazine over a period of years. The editors' opinions leaned heavily to rigidly conservative views which obviously had not conformed with majority opinions expressed by American voters through state and national elections. On the basis of this evidence, Obert argued, a majority of country editors were out of step with their readers and therefore an image they cherished of themselves as men of great influence was rapidly being dissipated. He charged that the editor is too often trying to meet today's problems by reciting, "Backward, turn backward, O Time in thy flight" rather than by trying to find out why things are changing and then acting on that knowledge to provide effective leadership. This is true, he said, of attitudes on both national problems and local affairs.

One of the most vitriolic responses to the Obert article came from Dwight Payton, former editor and publisher of the Overbrook (Kan.) *Citizen* and then an editorial writer for the Oklahoma City *Daily Oklahoman*. As reprinted in *The American Press* for September, 1959, part of his reply read:

If the whole of his lengthy diatribe . . . were epitomized, it would read like this: Most of the nation's country editors are bigoted moss-brains suffering from pre-Roosevelt arrested development and bemused by conceit sired by a myth about their political power. . . . This writer has been associated with the weekly press for over 20 years and came to know many publishers. . . . In all this time affiant never met a single editor who "shared the grand illusion." Though be it said a considerable number are gravely concerned with their nation's drift from freedom to regimentation following the New Deal blueprint so that they might well wish their power were greater. Obert's article is more revealing as a self-portrait of a so-called liberal than for anything said about country editors. . . . The typical country editor surely must offend the liberal view. He subscribes to such old-fashioned philosophies as the Ten Commandments, the teachings of Christ, and the Constitution of the United States. He believes in the dignity and glory of the individual and holds that the "social group" which is the liberals' great love is a soul-less monstrosity typified by communists. The country editor believes with religious fervor in free enterprise and he makes no apologies for his stand. It can be assumed that Obert holds contrary views which commit him to favor of regimented enterprise.[5]

Obert fired back in the November issue of the magazine, saying the editor he had described "does not offend me politi-

    [5] "Says 'Nieman Fellow' Portrays Country Editor as 'Moss-Brain,'" *The American Press,* September, 1959.

cally, Mr. Payton. He offends me professionally. I have chosen the country newspaper field for my career. I respect country newspapering and I want to see others respect it. I am deeply concerned that this respect will not be forth-coming as long as the 'typical country editor' clings to archaic, totally unrealistic and very often ludicrous attitudes and convictions as those attitudes and convictions relate to the great issues of our time."[6]

A more moderate critique came from Weimer Jones, editor of the Franklin (N.C.) *Press,* a past president of the North Carolina Press Association, who said ". . . there's enough truth in what he [Obert] says to warrant some soul-searching. For many of us, no doubt, are ill-informed, some of us, perhaps, stupid; a few of us, maybe, suffer from the environmental 'rigidity of rural ratiocination,' and all of us, collectively and individually, often are inconsistent . . . but . . . has the country press lost its influence that once enabled it to 'run the country?' . . . I'm inclined to doubt that because I don't think you can lose something you never had." He declared that it is certainly true that country editors go off in all directions—that Obert and Payton were prime examples of that truth—and that editors may be more fairly accused of underrating rather than overrating their influence, as witnessed by the fact that fewer than half of them run editorials and the "mild, sometimes almost apologetic tone of those they do run." He suspected that the country press reflects more public opinion than it molds and expressed skepticism about the validity of the polls on which the Obert article originally was based. He declared that in a time of meaningless labels and of doubt, he is convinced that "the country press has the greatest opportunity in its history. At a time when more and more people have less and less confidence in the daily press (with a few notable exceptions) and TV has discredited itself, the country press has become both a stabilizing influence and a dynamic, constructive force."[7]

When Editors Aren't "With It"

The most disquieting charge is that editors not only fail to provide editorial leadership in their communities but do not

---

[6] "Defends Harvard," *The American Press,* November, 1959.
[7] "Liberalism and the Country Press," *The Iowa Publisher,* November, 1960.

even reflect prevailing public opinion, nor do they have the perception to recognize what that opinion is. Ammunition for such charges was provided in a poll conducted by *The American Press,* in October, 1964, when it presented a pre-election poll on the Lyndon Johnson–Barry Goldwater race. The magazine made no claim that it was conducting scientific opinion sampling, of course, and presented the results only as an interesting bit of fuel for election debates. The ballots were on postcards inserted in the September issue, sent to 8,743 weeklies and to 1,311 dailies in the under-50,000-circulation bracket. More than 500 publishers from 46 states had returned the postcards by the time the results were compiled for the October issue, or a fairly respectable 5 per cent return.

It was no particular surprise or occasion for comment that the prevailingly conservative community newspaper publishers (except, rather surprisingly, in the New England area) preferred Senator Goldwater 60.6 per cent to 39.4 per cent for President Johnson. There was more reason for concern in the fact that 59.7 per cent said their areas *would vote* for Goldwater—and of course President Johnson won in a historic landslide. *Somebody* had to be indicating that they would vote for Johnson. It was not that Southern states carried a disproportionate weight in the straw ballot either, because the Middle Atlantic states, for instance, were declared to be favoring Goldwater 56–44, and the West North Central states were predicted to be dead even. If publishers can misjudge what their readers think and will do in such a dramatically wrong fashion, should they be entrusted with any leadership responsibilities? True, an editor can be in a small minority and still be "right" but that was not the question involved here; the question involved a judgment of what the editor expected *his area would do* in the election.

That this blindness, bordering on perversity, was not an accident of an unscientific poll, or an isolated case, was demonstrated by a poll among Wisconsin's weekly newspaper editors late in 1963 which showed almost unanimous opposition to President Johnson's Medicare proposal. Other opinion polls at the time showed public sentiment heavily in favor of Medicare. This was not the same thing as the presidential election poll, of course. Here many of the editors admitted they knew their readers favored Medicare, but they themselves still opposed it. This could amount to an even more shattering blow to the ego of the community weekly editor in that the reader must regard the paper with an amused, tolerant air, not really caring what the opinions are, prepared to go his own way regardless of the paper's editorial stands.

Other observers scoffed that the basis for the debate on editorial responsibility is irrelevant, insisting that a weekly newspaper stands or falls on its success as a *news* organ. As their proof they point to the long history of nonsuccess of publications devoted almost exclusively to opinion instead of to news. If examples are cited of journals which have won widespread notice as opinion leaders, the advocates of news content sort them into two classes: (1) publications which are reflections of individuals of great talent (such as a Harry Golden) and which do not survive in the same form long after the talent departs; or (2) papers which do an outstanding job in *both* news and comment.

Categorizing is complicated by the unmeasurable opinion ingredient added by vigorous news coverage. Surely if a community paper is deeply concerned with local social, economic, and political problems, as Obert urges, and covers these problems in depth, its stories may influence community opinion and action more directly and more decisively than a series of editorials would. Residents may need only to be fully informed about a source of water pollution, threatened loss of an industry, an incitement to juvenile delinquency, or some similar condition, to be impelled to action. The status conferral role of the press may, through thorough and consistent news coverage which is kept "objective" through the traditional forms of attribution, not only help readers identify the leaders to whom they may turn for direction to correct some condition, but may make the efforts of these leaders successful by rallying support behind them. Any good newsman can recount numerous instances where his news stories had quite unanticipated repercussions, sparking explosions of public opinion and action, just as he may also point to stories where he admittedly marshaled his evidence to support a particular point of view.

It may indeed be in the area of thorough news coverage where the true "power of the press" may lie for community weeklies. Does it really matter whether or not it is true that a congressman carefully assesses the opinion in his home district papers (as it is often claimed) before he votes on great national

questions, since he might never have won his seat had it not
been for the status conferred on him through news coverage of
his activities and his views in the hometown press of his district.

The News Plus the Editorial

Most effective of all is the combination of thorough news
reporting and the thoughtful, incisive editorial. When prizes
are awarded for community service, when recognition is given
to crusading editors, the achievements which have won the
honors have invariably resulted from this combination. No
clearer indication can be had that the American public still
accepts the following tenets as the true three-fold functions of
the newspaper: to serve as a marketing guide through its advertising columns; to inform through the news columns; and
to guide or lead through editorial comment.

Let's examine some of the publicly recognized examples
over the past decade. The Pulitzer Prize for editorial writing
went to small community newspapers for two successive years,
1963 and 1964. Ira Harkey, editor and publisher of the Pascagoula (Miss.) *Chronicle,* a weekly grown into a daily since he
purchased it in 1949, won the 1963 award for an editorial on
the disturbances at the University of Mississippi. The article
seemed a good step removed from fire-eating, and Harkey appeared to owe his award as much to an independence in reporting the news as to his editorial, which follows:

Anywhere else in the United States, the suggestion that a state university be closed down for any reason at all would not rise to the
level of public discussion. Such a suggestion could not originate
outside a lunatic academy.

But in our state—where the leaders for eight years led us to believe we would not be required to obey the same laws that others
must obey, whose leaders called out the mobs to let blood in sense-
less opposition to the will of the nation, where American GI's and
marshals are referred to in terms of hate formerly used only for
Huns who ravished Belgium in the World War and Japs who tor-
tured prisoners in World War II—in this state we had better discuss
the possibility. Now.

For the people who could do and say the things that have been
done and said in our state during the past six weeks have proved
themselves perfectly capable of closing down a university.

The suggestion has been made that Ole Miss be closed. It has been offered by the same group of false prophets who deluded the people for eight years into believing that we could maintain school segregation in Mississippi while all about us other Southern states were failing in their attempts to prevent integration. Somehow, in the face of all that is sane, they managed to convince most white people that they had a secret unknown to other Southern leaders.

If we now let them convince us that it is proper to close Ole Miss and destroy a century of cultural advancement, then maybe we do not deserve any better than to be led by owners of grammar-school intellects and of attitudes that most humans left behind somewhere in history.

It is heartening to note a resurgence of manhood on the part of the Ole Miss staff and faculty and the rallying of alumni support to keep the institution going. All alumni, all parents of present students, all Mississippians who care a hang about their state—we will exclude moral and religious considerations here and mention only the economic—all should also rally behind the university and let our leaders know that we do not regard suicide as a solution.[8]

The civil rights disputes of the past decade or more have tended to throw the spotlight on courageous attempts to maintain attitudes of independence and reason in sullen communities all too ready to accept redneck leadership and reject moderation. So it was that the next year's Pulitzer Prize for editorials went to Mrs. Hazel Brannon Smith, editor and publisher of the Lexington (Miss.) *Advertiser* and owner of three other weeklies near Lexington. Hers is a story of a long fight for fair and equitable law enforcement in the area served by her newspaper—a history of news stories backed by editorials about slot machine operators, liquor law violators, gamblers, and the corrupt local politicians who allowed vice to flourish. A story about the shooting of a Negro school teacher aroused the ire of the local White Citizens Council. Similar forthright coverage of racial incidents led to advertising boycotts, retaliation by her husband's employers, and threats of violence. Her prize-winning editorial, too, was notable for its moderation, though it protested firmly against the injustice of jailing a local Negro farmer on a charge of firebombing his own house in the middle of the night, then holding four other Negroes in jail for five days and nights in connection with the same incident before they were released for lack of evidence.

[8] Pascagoula (Miss.) *Chronicle,* November 9, 1962.

The Lovejoy Awards

Mrs. Smith has received a number of awards, one of the earliest being the 1960 Courage in Journalism Award given through Southern Illinois University in memory of the martyred abolitionist editor, Elijah P. Lovejoy. The Lovejoy awards are given for outstanding service involving courageous performance of duty in the face of economic, political, or social pressures against an editor by members of his own community. The purpose is stated as to encourage outspoken but responsible participation in local issues and controversies and to give credit where it is due for editorial leadership under conditions more rewarding to silence than to forthright printing of the facts. That there are always a number of worthy nominees for the honor each year is indeed powerful testimony that many weekly and small daily editors across the land do take seriously their responsibility to their communities; they bear no resemblance to an imaginary figure of a publisher cowed by his advertisers, a publisher who is lily-livered or moribund. Some of the Lovejoy winners in recent years show a variety of attitudes and approaches toward local responsibility (and varying degrees of success).

SAMUEL L. WOODRING (1961): Editor and publisher of the North Augusta (S.C.) *Star,* Woodring brought down upon himself the wrath of an important segment of his community for his stand on a shakeup in the police department. Perhaps a clue to the way resentment flared lies in the length of his residence in the community. A native of Pennsylvania who worked for Du Pont at the Savannah River Atomic Energy plant until 1954, he bought the name of a bankrupt weekly in North Augusta and had his little paper printed by contract for several years until he could assemble his own offset equipment. Still, it could not be the classic case of the outsider coming into an old, closely knit community because North Augusta was a boom town which expanded from 3,000 population to 10,000 in less than a decade. But a foundation for resentment was undoubtedly laid when he rose like a true journalist to the challenge of the city council's policy of closed meetings. His successful two-year fight to change the policy was recognized when he received the South Carolina Community Service

Award in 1959. However, in the fight which split the community he was on the side of the city council, which had accepted the resignation of the police chief after 35 years of service, and had dismissed the police sergeant. Woodring backed this action and the later hiring of a nonresident as police chief. Partisans of the two officers tried to organize an advertising boycott, made threatening telephone calls, and formed a mob which made it necessary for the Woodrings to have a police escort when they left the city hall after a council meeting. In the next municipal election the ticket supported by Woodring lost, and a group brought another weekly newspaper into the area to serve as an advertising competitor, but the net effect was to rally Woodring's supporters more strongly behind him, and he was able to maintain his paper.

Eugene H. (Gene) Wirges (1962): This long-continuing and extremely complicated case also involved a young (29) man who moved into a community hard-set in its political structure. Gene Wirges moved to Morrilton, Arkansas, in 1957 to take over two weeklies, the Morrilton *Democrat* and the *Perry County News*. Very quickly he learned that city and county offices were controlled by a highly effective political machine which saw to it that its candidates were returned to office in each election with the same 90 per cent margin of the votes cast. Wirges (there was an opposition weekly) first became involved in a contest with the machine when a group of farmers approached him for help in conducting a special recall election against three school board members in one section of the county. The insurgents won by a thirteen-vote margin, the enmity of the machine politicians toward the new editor was solidified, and in return Wirges began a series of investigative news reports about payroll padding, misappropriation of funds, and similar abuses. Editorially he called for a change to the city manager type of city government, but the plan lost in a referendum election. A news story following a township election in which the machine candidate got all but two out of ninety-five votes counted, and in which Wirges reported that the first fourteen voters interviewed all asserted they had voted for the losing candidate, brought a series of telephone threats, a shot fired near his head, and stones thrown at his home. A county official beat him, was fined $28.25, including costs, on a charge of assault. When he received the Lovejoy award, Wirges

told an interviewer that his foes had attempted to sell his paper
on an old judgment; to cut off his supplies through pressure on
suppliers; to bribe his employees; "but we are still there and
we are going to stay."

Time magazine covered the story in late 1961 but its sum-
mation proved to be unduly optimistic, "Thanks to the crusading country editor, the days when selection means election
in Conway County may be numbered."[9] In the summer of
1962, the Democratic primary election seemed to offer a little
hope that citizens were turning against the machine when the
county prosecuting attorney was defeated, but the political
bosses began a series of legal actions against Wirges. The editor
countered, with the result that he had pending before the November election: (1) a suit against the county official for damages because of the assault; (2) a suit against the sheriff (the machine boss) for $150,000; (3) another suit against the sheriff to
recover $528 in costs paid under protest in the matter of the
judgment; and (4) a suit against the opposition weekly for
$5,000 in libel damages.

In 1963 a county judge won a $200,000 judgment for libel
based on a column which Wirges said a woman volunteer correspondent had written, and the county clerk won libel
damages of $75,000. The judgments were appealed, and when
the costs of all this litigation together with losses in ad and circulation revenue made it appear that bankruptcy of the paper
was inevitable, a group of friendly creditors stepped in, bid in
the paper at a forced sale, and hired Wirges as editor. Later
the appeals court overturned the libel judgment won by the
judge, but a perjury charge grew out of the testimony, and in
February, 1966, Wirges was found guilty on that charge and
sentenced to three years in the penitentiary. The verdict was
appealed and the long fight continued. The Arkansas Supreme
Court reversed the $75,000 libel verdict won by the county
clerk. Wirges himself was free on bond awaiting the appeal,
but at the end of 1966 his wife was editing the paper and he
was reported dividing his time between his numerous legal
problems and the writing of a book on his experiences. In mid-
1967 the last of the criminal charges against him were dismissed.

---

[9] "Varieties of Violence," *Time*, September 22, 1961.

W. PENN JONES, JR. (1963): National attention was focused on the small town of Midlothian, Texas (population 1,500), when a firebomb was tossed through the office window of the weekly *Mirror,* and it culminated in the Lovejoy award to an editor whose view of his mission was that he should make residents of his community "realize the duties that went along with their rights as citizens." (His opposition said he came to town angry in 1946 and stayed that way.) Jones purchased the *Mirror* after leaving the Army with the rank of major. He had no previous newspaper experience, but very quickly stirred up the old town by his insistence on covering the town council and school board meetings. A long-running feud with the school superintendent simmered for years, and the violence exploded in 1962 over the editor's opposition to scheduling in the school speakers with the viewpoint held by the John Birch Society, without granting equal time to speakers representing an opposition point of view. Jones became involved in fisticuffs with the school principal and with the self-acknowledged John Birch speaker. The editor and the principal both paid fines for their scuffle. The bomb thrown into the newspaper office caused damaged estimated at $4,000, but the bomber couldn't be found.

Jones again flashed into national prominence in 1966 when a series of articles he had been running in his newspaper on his theories about the Kennedy assassination were compiled in a small book and met a widespread response. His theory of a conspiracy got more circulation when it was picked up and elaborated by the magazine *Ramparts* in its November, 1967, issue.

SIDNEY CURTIS (1966): A different picture is to be seen in the 1966 award, in that the editor had been a resident of his city for thirty years and the town had the shifting population of a resort city. Curtis had a background as a big city daily reporter before he bought, in 1936, a struggling little 265-circulation weekly in Revere, Massachusetts. He built it into a thriving business, outlasting three competitive weeklies. His is a story of a long struggle against corrupt municipal administration, some victories, some losses, but enough success to gain the newspaper rather solid support from substantial citizens. In one of the most recent "down cycles" in 1964, Curtis told an audience at the Lovejoy award presentation, "one of the new councilmen came into my office. He told me there was plenty of money to be made in the new administration. This is when I was offered the $100,000. I told him I wasn't interested. He asked me if I was interested in power. He said I could have my say who was appointed to certain boards. I said I wasn't interested in power, either. All I was interested in was good government."[10]

An opposition weekly was soon started and was given the city's legal advertising. Curtis began to receive telephoned threats and the front window of his printing plant was smashed eleven times in the next two years. His advertisers reported they were pressured and Curtis was made defendant in a libel suit for $250,000 by one of the city commissioners. Elections in 1964 and 1965 changed the form of city government and elected a new mayor, and apparently Revere then entered one of its "up cycles" of good government.

J. A. NEWBORN, JR. (1967): The time-honored watchdog and investigative role of the community press was exemplified in the 1967 award to the publisher of the Clear Lake City (Texas) *Suburban Journal*. Newborn spent several months in an investigation of rumored irregularities in the financial operations of a school district in the paper's area. The superintendent resigned and the matter became the central issue in a hotly contested school board election. The *Suburban Journal*'s support of one slate led to an attempt to organize a boycott on advertising in the paper. Newborn received threatening telephone calls, the windshield of his car was broken, and a missile was thrown through a window at his home.[11]

Every State Has Crusaders

Every state, it should be clear, can offer examples of fearless editors. They are the obvious answer to the occasional plaintive query, "Where are the great crusading newspapers we had in the past?" The Lovejoy committee turns up dozens of

---

[10] "Municipal Crusader Wins Courage Award," *Editor & Publisher*, July 23, 1966.
[11] "Weekly Publisher Lovejoy Winner," *Publishers' Auxiliary*, July 29, 1967.

them, and their courage is just as fiery as it was during any of the great disputes of our history—abolition of slavery, free-soil, populism, coal strikes, or the many other occasions in which regional or national passions ran high.

It is especially easy to stir up local controversy over "the right to know." An idealistic editor comes into a long-settled community which is pretty self-satisfied with "the way we get along" and offers to report for his readers all the details of the way their units of government function. He receives some encouragement; the thought seems fully in consonance with the democratic way. He therefore charges into the fray with a whoop and a holler, but when he glances behind for his support troops he finds them squatted on their haunches a safe distance to the rear. Indeed, as he demands open meetings and open records he finds that veteran officials, set in their habits of agreeing on policies in private, have large coteries of supporters (the ones who keep re-electing them) who tend to agree that "there's no sense hurting people's feelings," and "no one is going to speak out if it's going to be spread all over the paper." So the editor finds his position on the battlefield is a lonely one. Many at this point will fall back and regroup, seeking their ends through diplomacy rather than sheer firepower. Others who do not change tactics may win awards but lose their businesses or decide to seek new locations. A few winners carry their communities along with them.

The large group of editors that either rejects open combat or believes that ends can be attained through subtler means may be represented by Tom O'Connor, editor of the Allendale (S.C.) *Country Citizen,* who wrote to *Publishers' Auxiliary* in 1965:

It could be envy, of course. . . . I just wonder. Every now and then when I read of these crusading editors who win prizes for noble stands on controversial questions, many of short life and little merit, I think I detect a phony ring somewhere in the sound of the words. What's the point in alienating friends and ruining your influence? Instead of fighting the other fellow's viewpoint why not try to understand it? After all he's like you, a church-going citizen of some integrity, capable of honest emotion, concern for his fellow man and anxious that peace and order should govern his days.

And why is it that those editors who are really guilty of stirring things up (often to no good purpose) are the fewest and not always the sincerest of the editors in their locale? Is it to be taken as

axiomatic, that men elected to public office, to city hall, the courthouse, or the legislature, are per se crooks and highbinders? That
the fellow who does not agree with you on questions of politics,
economics, or race relations, is always and forever wrong? To take
a stand is one thing, to be right is another. Nobody's crooked in
my town. The boys at city hall are doing a frequently thankless
job, as well as they can. The courthouse crowd does the job required. Who's crooked? For that matter, who's completely honest?
Prizes for standing off the mobs, dodging the bullets, creating dis-
sension and trouble? Bushwa, I say. Where are yesterday's prize-
winners now?

A correspondent who classified himself as a "crusading
editor" replied that "a newspaper that sees nothing at all times
but sweetness and light is either circulating within a utopian
community, or else it hasn't the energy or desire to ask questions."

A Profit With Honor

Changing economic conditions have always had a bearing
and may have much more influence in the future. Professor J.
Edward Gerald, his perception of the small town newspaper
sharpened by substantial experience as manager of the Missouri
Press Association, contended that, "The basic goal professed by
newspaper owners is to operate at a profit with honor. They
have many other related goals and values, . . . but profitable
operation—or lack of it—governs the degree and the kind of
attention the newspapers can give to any other consideration."
He explained that this consideration governs any size or type
of newspaper operation, but the effect on the idealistic values of
the small community newspaper publisher is much more immediate and direct. At the smallest levels he must handle many
duties himself, because his income does not allow him to engage much help, and most of these duties involve production.
"The difference in the orientation of the publisher and his non-
journalistic critics is greatest at this point," Gerald writes, "for
it is here, particularly, that the task of the critic is to manipulate
words, while the publisher must manipulate people—customers
and employees—to get the desired results. The critics have developed the concept of social responsibility to help put pressure
on the private entrepreneur at the moment when he is evaluat-

ing their proposals for reform. As the publisher would certainly point out, the critic would expect him to finance, at his own risk, the recommended controversial public policy information campaigns and extensive additions of content in support of cultural objectives . . . assume a reformer's role which would put him in conflict with important parts of the community."[12]

The sharp swing to centralized printing, not only in the form of group publication which we find in the suburbs but the cooperative enterprises springing up in rural areas, will change the editor's enforced concentration on production problems (though it won't necessarily decrease financial risks involved in conflicts with parts of the community). His other goals and values may then receive more attention. Our summaries of the activities of "courage-in-journalism" award winners demonstrated that news stories were the basic ingredients of their campaigns. It takes time, much time, to study financial records or legal documents, to attend long drawn-out meetings, to interview persons involved in a controversy, to check and recheck the facts to insure the accuracy without which any crusade falls flat on its face. An editor whose operation demands a large share of his time for such production activities as typesetting and presswork (or even selling advertising and job printing) either must draw the time from his in-depth reporting, or pay for the time used in reporting by unbalancing his financial stability.

Work done in the central plant is not free, of course, and the business side of the small paper will always demand close attention to pay the costs of production, wherever the work is done. Publishers have been exhorted for decades to value their own time more highly, to pay others the lesser rate required for purely mechanical tasks, and to concentrate their efforts on the more professional activities which should merit a higher rate of compensation. This philosophy has meaning only if the editor and publisher work *effectively* at the more professional level, and thereby increase the income of the enterprise. The central plant at least gives them the *opportunity* (and some incentive) to do that.

For it is clear that the responsibilities which society, by general if somewhat tacit agreement, has assigned to the community newspaper editor bear as heavily in areas of what he fails or

---

[12] *The Social Responsibility of the Press* (Minneapolis: University of Minnesota Press, 1963).

refuses to do as in what he does do. He may be accused of apathy when really his failures result from the way economic burdens force him to apportion his time. He may fail to offer editorial comment on the grounds that he lacks adequate background, but he does not study issues because physical activity in production work exhausts both his time and his energy. The feeling for objectivity ingrained in the newsman wars against the crusader's impulse, the desire to win a point by presenting it in the most favorable light possible. As the enemies of Henry J. Raymond, founder of the New York *Times,* called him a "trimmer," so his friends found his ability to see both sides of troublesome questions as his greatest journalistic virtue. It take little time to come to a quick decision when information is scanty; it is far harder to make that decision when the evidence is voluminous and takes time for study. And it may take even more time when information is hard to obtain.

Although some naturally disagree, most editors believe that political office is not the most satisfactory route to community influence and prestige. Rather, they see office-holding (and many would extend this even to appointive offices) as tending to compromise their independence and objectivity. That was a point made vigorously by Clayton Rand, a Mississippi editor who served as president of the National Editorial Association:

. . . it has been my observation that an editor usually loses what little influence he has as a publisher when he becomes a candidate. It is then that he compromises with his convictions, and from the day he begins seeking political office men look between the lines of everything he writes for the hidden and ulterior motive. . . . The chief satisfaction of being a country editor is that one is free. He may not always be prosperous, but there is no wealth that can compensate for placing a mortgage on one's conscience.[13]

Giving the editor more time for in-depth reporting and for thoughtful editorial comment does not thereby assure effective community leadership. The gatekeeper function operates in still another way. Given the same amount of information, or equal access to it, one editor may fail to perceive any value or interest in it, another may develop an aspect which his readers regard as a sensation. These differences in perception, however,

---

[13] *Ink on My Hands* (New York: Carrick & Evans, 1940).

operate at all levels and in all areas, not just the journalistic; they are the same differences that make for horse races and the political races. Still and all, the editor's most precious commodity is time, and if the newer technology will give him more of that it cannot help but improve the chances of the community press for survival over the long range. But more than survival, society demands positive contributions and it expects more of its leaders than a record of past performance; it counts what it believes could or should have been done. Browning said it in his *The Lost Leader:*

> We shall march prospering—not through his presence;
>   Songs may inspirit us—not from his lyre;
> Deeds will be done—while he boasts his quiescence,
>   Still bidding crouch whom the rest bade aspire;
> Blot out his name then, record one lost soul more,
>   One task more declined, one more footpath untrod. . . .

Where the advocates of the moderate, let's-talk-it-over approach part from the crusaders is in their evaluation of the intensity of the demand from the community for leadership. "Need ALL the footpaths be trods?" they ask. Most of the problems of the modern community are fragmented; they lend themselves well to study and treatment from small activist groups with a special interest. In the long run acceptable priorities are established and the necessary accommodations or trade-offs are made. All will agree that progress perhaps should be greater and faster, but most will be satisfied with small gains. As I. F. Stone said in discussing the ultimate decline of revolutionary movements, ". . . it is because man, still half-monkey, cannot live at so high a pitch, and when the bugles die down, prefers a quiet scratch in the warm sun."

Chapter 8

THEY CLAMOR TO BE HEARD

"THE WEEKLY BUSINESS is often so difficult that it defies description," wrote William Keifer in *The Gannetteer,* publication of Gannett Newspapers, Incorporated, in explaining why he gave up his role as weekly newspaper editor and publisher after six years to return to the staff of a daily newspaper.

A correspondent wrote in to agree that the hours needed to publish a small weekly make it almost prohibitive, and added, "After seven years in the bussiness I know of no way to lick the economics of the business."[1]

In contrast a 1961 interview in *Editor & Publisher* recounted that Frank Hash, an Iowa publisher and owner of a community radio station, was retiring to return to college and study for a master's degree. "How many big city reporters or editors have the money to retire at 39?" he is quoted as asking.[2]

A letter in the *Texas Press Messenger* gave a first-person account of the experiences of a journalism graduate who had first been employed as editor of a weekly, then owned one himself for seventeen months. He decided it wasn't worth the long hours, the meetings, the endless variety of duties a newsman is called upon to perform, and the financial sacrifice. Newspapering seemed to be a one-way street. It seemed the community

---

[1] A more complete version of Keifer's article ("So You Want to Own a Weekly" appeared in *Saturday Review,* May 14, 1966; the responding letter appeared in *Saturday Review,* July 9, 1966.

[2] Martha Nelson, "Success, and Money, Too," *Editor & Publisher,* September 2, 1961.

demanded everything and gave very little in return. So he left and went to work as a copywriter in a San Antonio advertising agency.

In rebuttal, Shelby V. Candland of the Walden (Colo.) *Jackson County Star* wrote that he came into the weekly field with no previous experience after living in a big city (Denver) and "after two years of twelve to eighteen hours daily, I find no other profession that is as exciting, fun-giving and exhilarating as working in a country weekly shop." He found a real value in working for himself and wondered if young people of this country aren't losing their spirit to pioneer.

Which is the truer picture? Well, as the man says, it all depends. Similar contrasts and comparisons between success and failure, satisfaction and discontent, staying in and getting out, can be found in all occupations and all types of business or even the professions. A dentist (a good one) quits the profession to become a salesman, teachers quit to operate stores, journalism history is full of lawyers who became editors, and so on. And what do all the examples prove? Nothing. For the weekly press they aren't intended to prove anything. They are offered to show that the breed still has vitality, that it is still evolving, that the process of natural selection is still at work, that as the environment changes the organism can still adapt to it.

Which Type Will Survive?

The preceding chapters have traced the development of the weekly newspaper and some of the changes it has been and is undergoing. It is time to consider the almost endless mutations which, as in nature, sometimes succeed but more often fail, and to try to determine what the strain of the future is to be.

In a special issue of *Grassroots Editor,* examining the current status of the weekly press, Professor Kenneth Byerly asserted the future of weeklies, taken as a whole, is brighter than ever before, and cited as proof "the ever-growing dollar volume they gross," and that "weekly paid circulation in 1962 set a record-breaking high (24,399,490) for the ninth straight year." He said the long decline in number of units had stopped, that the number of weeklies in the United States has remained almost stable in recent years.[3]

It has already been noted that small weeklies in villages of less than 1,000 population have continued to drop off at a steady rate and that their decline has been offset by the number of new papers started in the suburbs. This doesn't mean that there no longer are any new "small town" weeklies being started; occasionally a little community gets a new injection of economic vigor because a new plant is built, or a dam is constructed, or some hitherto ignored natural resource is tapped. About the first thing such a community wants, if it hasn't got one, is its "own" newspaper. In the face of a declining enthusiasm among young people coming out of journalism schools for life in the small town (a trend of much concern to many professions and industry besides the newspaper business), where do the editors and publishers come from not only to replace the natural attrition caused by retirement or death, but to man the new units which are started?

Some Varied Examples

Despite the frequent groans heard from an older generation about the current preoccupation of young people with security, the desire to "be my own boss" is still a very real and widespread motivating force. It is the reason, admitted or not, why the story of the big city newspaperman becoming a weekly publisher has become a stereotype. Those in the business properly scoff at the "I'm going to get away from all the pressure, have more time to hunt and fish," comments because only a very few could be that naïve if they are true newsmen. Those few are quickly disabused of notions of less pressure and more time for loafing. A few examples will suffice to show the great variety of ways new blood is continually infused into the community newspaper field.

Owen K. Ball at forty-seven left a job as managing editor of the Miami (Fla). *News* to buy the weekly Evergreen (Colo.) *Canyon Courier*. He had some initial doubts when he found

[3] "The Future of America's Weeklies," *Grassroots Editor*, July, 1963.

himself working faster, harder, and longer than he had on the big daily, and because he had to be primarily a businessman rather than the reporter and writer he had envisioned himself to be. But after he had time to organize the operation, make the many changes and improvements he felt were required, he could say, "This has been the most satisfying job of my life. And it's been fun—and profitable. Would I do it again? I'd love to!" In an interview with Rick Friedman of *Editor & Publisher* he had some advice for other daily newspapermen who might entertain the dream of owning their own newspaper:

I think there are many fine daily newspapermen who could succeed in the weekly newspaper field. And I think the weekly field would benefit from these people getting into it. But there are qualifications. Operating a weekly is a job for a businessman, and the best editor in the world could go broke on most weeklies if he doesn't watch the dollars. A newsman should, therefore, have at least an understanding of business practices and be willing to attend to business. . . .

The problem for transplanting daily to weekly newspapermen is *people*. In the daily, the reporter deals with a high percentage of strangers; in the small town he knows, personally, every newsmaker. This has to make a difference in handling stories, and requires a great deal more tact if the essence of the story is to appear. The bull-in-a-china-shop reporter won't last long in the small town; nor will the editor who moves in and makes a fetish of attacking advertisers or established institutions to prove he's got guts. He may have the latter but he won't have a newspaper very long. At the same time I see no reason to knuckle under, suppress news, kowtow to advertisers, or otherwise do anything that compromises principles. Newspapering is newspapering, wherever it is practiced.[4]

Horace V. Wells, editor and publisher of the Clinton (Tenn.) *Courier-News,* winner in 1957 of the second Elijah P. Lovejoy Award for Courage in Journalism, recalls that he left a large daily in the 1930's to start his own weekly, though he had never worked on one. In a sense he found that an advantage, in that he did things he didn't know couldn't be done. He, too, found the satisfaction that comes in the personal relationships—though sometimes these involve some personal peril. "On a small community newspaper, no matter who writes what, the readers give credit to the man out front . . . the editor and

---

[4] "Ex-Daily Man," in "The Weekly Editor," *Editor & Publisher,* October 16, 1965.

publisher. . . . As far as the readers were concerned, what was said was my opinion. . . . In larger cities the editors can be anonymous, but not in Clinton. When subscribers, or those who borrowed the paper, didn't like what was said they didn't get pen and paper to write a letter. They started hunting for the editor!"

In time, he found, residents came to expect his column to take a stand on every local issue, telling him they might not always agree but that much of the time he was right. Thus he felt his paper and his personal opinion column are doing a job in which he can take satisfaction "creating comment, making people think, getting action and helping make ours a better community. Why make a change and take a chance on losing this?"[5]

THORNE LANE, editor and manager of the Hogansville (Ga.) *Troup County Herald,* fired back at those professing to be disillusioned by a difference in monetary rewards between work on the big city daily and a small town weekly. He advised beginners that if they are "selfish, enter advertising . . . if unselfish he can be [on the editorial side] of more service to his fellow man than in any other profession." He asserted that he had had experience on both sides and that he worked at a higher salary as a daily newspaper ad man than as a daily newspaper editor. However, he "bought a controlling interest in a weekly, [and] I pay myself more than twice as much as I was ever paid as editor of a daily and perform a greater service to my fellow man."[6]

'Retiring' to the Country. Rick Friedman of *Editor & Publisher,* in his column "The Weekly Editor," described in a series of personality sketches the experiences of several former big city newsmen. ALAN G. NICHOLAS[7] was a Hearst executive in Pittsburgh who decided after sale of the *Sun-Telegraph* there to try out some long-held ideas on his own community newspaper. He took over the *Tribune* at Liberty, Mo., now a tri-weekly, and began a vigorous program to sharpen the news coverage but

[5] "Not-So-Quiet Weekly," in "The Weekly Editor," *Editor & Publisher,* November 14, 1964.
[6] "Voice of Experience" in "Letters to the Editor," *Editor & Publisher,* February 5, 1966.
[7] "Editor from Big Town," in "The Weekly Editor," *Editor & Publisher,* September 21, 1963.

also to give the newspaper a positive editorial image. He printed an editorial platform, began to endorse candidates for political office, became involved in a campaign supporting a bond issue for a local hospital, and otherwise took specific positions. He felt the community endorsed his efforts when both advertising volume and his circulation doubled in the first year.

After ten years as a printer on a Dallas daily, J. R. FREE-MAN bought a 600-circulation weekly, the Frederick (Colo.) *Farmer and Miner,* twenty-five miles north of Denver. Although he was without training on the editorial side, the chance to express his own opinion was really what he sought in the new venture and he "deeply resents the fact that I cannot spend more time in editorial writing." This is the case even though his editorials and his personal column have often stirred bitter resentment among local officials who think his suggestions for local improvements are personal shafts aimed at them. He and his wife have received "nasty" anonymous telephone calls and an effort was made to organize an advertising boycott but there are enough compensating aspects to "give our life meaning and purpose. . . . As long as this country remains free and the press remains free . . . we will stay in business as long as we can put a meal on the table."[8]

Freeman gained national prominence during 1966–67 for his crusade to block private exploitation of rich oil shale lands in Colorado and Utah owned by the federal government. A report of his efforts in *Editor & Publisher*[9] drew a letter from Stewart L. Udall, Secretary of the Interior, which presented the Department's case and disputed a number of Freeman's assertions.[10] Freeman replied in a letter to the magazine which presented ten points that Freeman said the Secretary "implicitly admitted or has not denied." The first point of the list of ten seems to sum up the extent of the basic charges and also highlights the difficulties a crusading editor may face: "(1) The purchase of politicians by oil shale claimants and oil companies, the deliberate ousting of public-minded federal employees, threats, intimidations, and the attempted murder of this editor."[11]

---

[8] "Ex-Daily Man and Wife," in "The Weekly Editor," *Editor & Publisher,* October 23, 1965.
[9] "The Weekly Editor," *Editor & Publisher,* July 1, 1967.
[10] "Letters to the Editor," *Editor & Publisher,* July 29, 1967.
[11] "Letters to the Editor," *Editor & Publisher,* September 2, 1967.

Freeman was credited with an impressive victory in May, 1968, when stories out of Washington, D.C., reported that the Department of the Interior had wiped out 5,200 mining claims in the oil shale region. Freeman's view was that this was only a partial victory and that he intended to continue his efforts to curb the exploiters. In the meantime, however, the time and expense he had devoted to his investigations had forced him to sell his little paper. In the sales agreement it was specified that he would continue as associate editor, with freedom to continue publishing his oil shale investigation articles. Now the once-obscure country editor was being visited by reporters for big metropolitan newspapers and national magazines who were seeking use of his documentary evidence for their own investigations of the oil shale problem.

Freeman told an interviewer he was "dead broke," and that after the sale of his paper he had no plans pending the outcome of his application for a Nieman Fellowship at Harvard. "If I don't get a Nieman, the next alternative is to put together the best resumé I can dream up and go out looking for a job. But with my record of hell-raising, I don't even know where to start."[12]

None of these examples indicates that the persons entering the weekly field were motivated by an interest in politics, either to use the paper as a base from which to run for and hold office, or to support a particular ideology. Yet this *should* be a reason for young people to enter the field, argues John C. Obert, the Minnesota editor whose article, critical of the community press for its lack of interest in exerting editorial influence, was mentioned previously. Following up his original article, Obert reviewed the obvious evidence for the political one-sidedness of the press and said he believed something ought to be, and could be, done about it.

A good many [hometown] newspapers . . . are for sale for a price. And, despite the political myth to the contrary, there are liberals who have money, money which conceivably could be used to purchase or finance purchase of erstwhile conservative newspapers. Why haven't liberals purchased newspapers as conservatives have? I would suspect a combination of factors. In the first place, of course, there is the overriding fact that there are simply fewer liberals with

---

[12] "Oil Shale Crusader," in "The Weekly Editor," *Editor & Publisher*, May 18, 1968. Freeman did not get a 1968–69 Nieman Fellowship.

money than conservatives with money. In the second place, it would seem to me that liberal money, if we choose to call it that, is located primarily in metropolitan centers, and the purchase of a metropolitan daily is a far different matter than the purchase of a country weekly. . . . It is my belief that liberals with available money simply have not been alerted to the possibilities inherent in the ownership or control of small newspapers. . . . And while I am unalterably opposed to political party ownership of newspapers or even the financing of newspaper purchase, I can see no reason why the party cannot serve as an informal broker or why prominent party figures cannot serve as the catalyst to bring together liberal money and liberal newspapermen who want to own or operate liberal newspapers.[13]

He contends there is a large pool of trained newspapermen who would be interested in such opportunities but who have little chance, in these high income tax days, of accumulating the capital needed to purchase newspapers, or at any rate those of a size sufficient to have a good chance of commercial success.

But There Are Other "Communities." If there's a lack of interest in reverting to the political party paper of an earlier day, there's no absence of new papers founded to meet other specialized interests and considerations. There are many "communities" defined by other than geographical boundaries, and there are always entrepreneurs ready to offer a service to meet the demand, supposed or real, of these communities for a "voice."

The strong foreign-language press which flourished in the melting-pot era of our national history and which produced fortunes for a good number of skillful publishers, is now pretty much confined to a few large cities, but its place is being taken by other special interest publications.

The Negro Press. The Negro press, for instance, has been enjoying rapid growth, although by the very nature of things at present it is concentrated in the metropolitan areas and need not now be considered as an aspect of the small town press. The thirteenth annual survey of the Negro press made by the Department of Journalism of Lincoln University in Missouri,

---

[13] "What About Weeklies?" *Nieman Reports*, July, 1961. Obert has since resigned as editor of the Alexandria (Minn.) *Park Region Echo* to enter federal government public relations work.

released at the end of 1966, shows 172 papers intended for Negro audiences, with a total circulation of nearly 2,000,000. This was a dramatic increase of thirty-nine newspapers and more than 400,000 in circulation in the two years since the previous survey in 1964. A breakdown shows papers in thirty-six states and the District of Columbia, with seventeen in California, fourteen in New York, and eleven in Texas. We may see in the not-too-distant future, with the advantages offered by simplified composition equipment and centralized printing and with an improved economic status and increased self-awareness of the Negro, a development of a true small town press serving the Negro in the South. This awaits, of course, some significant development of a retail trading class among the Negroes.

Court and Commercial Press. Another form of a "community" press, which appears to be little known to the average citizen even though of impressive size, is the group of court and financial newspapers which serve judges, attorneys, brokers, commodity dealers, real estate firms, and many similar business and professional men. These papers, too, by their very nature are concentrated in the larger cities where legal and financial activities are centered. Most of the publications are weeklies, but directories list 76 dailies, and a trade group, Associated Court and Commercial Newspapers, brings members together regularly for discussion of mutual problems. These newspapers are highly specialized in that their news content deals almost exclusively with statistical information, real estate transfers, bid notices and awards, court decisions, real estate and chattel mortgage listings, etc., while most of their revenue is derived from "public notice"—the official proceedings of legal bodies, the notices required in probate proceedings, calls for bids, and similar "legals" which are familiar to all newspaper publishers. The court and commercial newspapers thrive in the big cities for two basic reasons: (1) they concentrate a type of content in a way which makes it more convenient for a specialized audience of attorneys, real estate dealers, brokers, etc.; and (2) the metropolitan dailies do not seek the "public notice" advertising because the maximum rates set by state statute are well below even the minimum line rate the newspaper gets for its advertising space.

Though these newspapers do not circulate to general

audiences, they can on occasion be effective movers of public opinion, through either special news articles or editorial opinion or both, because their readers are persons of great influence in the business and legal circles of a community. It is interesting to speculate on the mutations which may develop among newspapers of this classification as the ferment in American urban life continues to bubble and new forms of metropolitan organization develop.

One reaction to the extension of metropolitan newspaper capital and influence into the suburbs may be through establishment of such court newspapers printed in the suburban plants, perhaps developing a hybrid which will challenge the metropolitans sharply for certain forms of national advertising, and stressing a broader spectrum of news about the core city.

Church-Oriented Press. Religion provides another community of interest, and there are several hundred church-oriented and church-connected weeklies which get mixed into the statistics and often help to show a higher number of papers and a larger total circulation for the "community press" than is really justified. The Catholic Press Directory lists more than 130 Catholic newspapers in the country. These almost without exception serve a larger geographical area than a town or city; most of them represent a diocese. There are two national Catholic weeklies which publish a number of regional editions.

Professor James W. Carty, Jr., a former daily newspaper religion editor, finds the Protestant press so varied and diverse that it is hard to separate out a portion which might be analogous to the community weekly. "The different types of publications," he notes, "are occasioned by the particular needs, aims, and resources of denominations at the local, state, and national levels. Circulation may be city-wide, nation-wide, or world-wide; readership may be largely denominational or interdenominational. Weeklies may be categorized according to several types. First, are the general purpose publications that are read by many readers of different interests. Included are: (a) the non-denominational periodical and (b) the denominational weekly published by a congregation, a state church organization, or a regional or national religious body. Second, the special purpose weeklies, which are oriented toward one particular public, as the Sunday School papers."[14]

[14] "Protestant Weeklies," *Grassroots Editor,* July, 1963.

It is plain that religious newspapers are not competitive to the community press, except to the trivial extent that they take a tiny slice from the advertising dollar of either a local business or a national advertiser, and it is difficult to see any metamorphosis such papers would undergo which would move them to any extent into the field now occupied by the community weekly.

The Shopper or "Throwaway." The kind of publication which may start out drawing little attention, pass through several stages of development, and emerge as a serious challenger to the hometown newspaper is the "shopper" or "throwaway" referred to in a previous chapter. In its final stage, of course, it may become a true newspaper, thus adding to the total strength of the community press, or at worst, just displacing a weaker unit.

It would be interesting to try to trace the earliest beginnings of this kind of publication, but it is certain to be a most difficult, if not impossible, task because copies and files of these advertising sheets are not preserved in the way newspapers have been. No one (not even Gluttz himself) seems to have an impulse to save a shopper with a doubletruck ad of the Gluttz Department Store in the same way that families saved an edition telling of the death of McKinley or the story of the World War I Armistice.

It is certain, however, that the Great Depression of the 1930's gave the shoppers an impetus which has carried them along to the present day. At a time when millions were jobless, many devised whatever ways they could to scratch out a living. Selling advertising in a period of depression might now seem to be a paradoxical way of seeking to become self-employed, because it certainly is true that a beleaguered merchant often sees his advertising budget as the easiest place to cut expense. Yet it was also true that in this period the average retailer was fighting desperately to maintain some volume of business, and whenever someone offered a medium which not only promised to extend coverage beyond his normal range but do it at lower prices the retailer was interested. The promoter of the shopper sought only to make a bare living and was content with a meager return for the time he spent. At the same time printers searching for business were interested in taking on the publication as a printing job more to keep their shops busy than to turn a profit. Improvements in duplicating machines have now made it practical for owners of these little publications to bypass printers altogether, and with the aid of family members to do all the production work—lettering advertisements, typing stencils, running the duplicator, assembling the sheets, and delivering the paper.

If It Happens Again . . .

I would advance a theory here that if the United States falls again into an economic depression, or even a major recession, and a large number of newspaper or advertising employees are thrown out of work, we will see another big surge of "shoppers." Modern equipment makes one-man or family operations more feasible than ever before, and if a man is jobless for a considerable period of time he will be content with a slim margin of profit to supplement unemployment benefits, welfare checks, or similar income. Persons with a professional news background will not be content to produce a sheet filled entirely with advertising; they will add news and editorial content. Eventually some of these throwaways will emerge as true newspapers, finding for themselves a hitherto unoccupied niche in the community. It is unlikely, of course, that we will ever again see anything matching the Great Depression of the Thirties, but even a moderate decline from our present level of affluence will seem relatively severe.

Convention proceedings of national and state newspaper associations in the 1930's, and the *Service Letter* of the National Editorial Association frequently contained exchanges of advice among publishers for meeting the new competition. The *Service Letter* for June, 1931, carried an item which began, "Weekly newspapers in a number of cities of from three to five thousand population . . . have had to face a new form of competition in recent months in the form of a daily mimeographed sheet. Reports received by the N.E.A. show that in some cities these mimeographed dailies are not getting anywhere and are not considered a serious threat; from other cities comes a different version which indicates they are no joke and have the newspaper worried."

A Colorado publisher reported that his solution was to buy out the competitor and then keep issuing the "daily reminder" on his own presses each day except the day his weekly was published. A North Dakota publisher said he had found a successful solution in converting his weekly to a tabloid daily, but acknowledged that a community would have to be of adequate size and "ready" for such a step. Where the field would not be large enough he suggested that "a farm paper weekly with a lower subscription price but covering a larger area is the answer." Apparently he meant a companion publication for the regular weekly, and in effect he seemed to be advocating a form of the auxiliary shopping publication so common today in the community weekly field.

The editor of the *NEA Service Letter*, Herman Roe of Northfield, Minnesota, who won the accolade of "Mr. Country Editor" for his long and devoted service to the national association and to the field generally, noted in the *Service Letter* that his own community was threatened with this form of competition. "During the past two months two strangers appeared in Northfield . . . opened an office here and announced they would launch a mimeographed daily." However, the advertising committee of the town's Retail Merchants Association sent a letter to members which advised that "The so-called publication lacks evidence of permanency; it appears to be another plan for taking money out of town; and it would obviously be an expensive, although cheap-appearing type of advertising."[15] Roe urged other editors to work closely with their merchants to discourage invading publications, although where *local* residents were involved, the devastating argument that "it takes money out of town" could not be used and weekly publishers had to find other ways to combat shoppers.

One defense which had a widespread spate of popularity before adverse court decisions cut it down[16] was to work through the local municipal government for passage of an "anti-handbill" ordinance. One such law which was passed in a number of communities and recommended for others provided that "No person shall distribute, cast, throw, or place any handbill, poster bill, show bill, dodger, circular pamphlet or any advertisement in or upon any street, sidewalk, alley or

[15] *NEA Service Letter*, National Editorial Association, St. Paul, Minn. July, 1932.
[16] See Frank Thayer, *Legal Control of the Press* (4th ed.; Brooklyn: The Foundation Press, 1962).

public place in (name of city), or in or upon any yard, porch, step or steps, on the premises of any other person in (name of city) . . . provided . . . not construed to interfere with or restrain the distributing of . . . newspapers, as defined by the Laws of (name of state)."

These ordinances were urged as anti-littering measures, although the sentiment against litter then was mild as compared to the concern of the present day. Publications could still be sent through the mails to each householder, of course, but the theory was that addressing and postage costs might just prove to be the item that would kill a close-margin operation.

To further assure that these costs would be markedly more than the two-bits for which a boy would gladly deliver a hundred or so papers house to house, the newspapers obtained a favorable ruling from the Post Office Department. An order dated July 7, 1934, amended Section 520, Postal Laws and Regulations, by adding: "Provided, That publications produced by the stencil, mimeograph, or hectograph process, or in imitation of typewriting, shall not be regarded as printed within the meaning of this clause." Postmasters were informed that "it will be seen that alleged periodical publications of this kind are not admissible as second-class matter."

. . . Or the Retailers Enter

A form of free distribution publication which aroused intense but short-lived concern was discussed in the September, 1933, issue of *Tide,* an advertising magazine. It discussed a plan under which regional managers of Sears, Roebuck & Company were allowed to start free distribution Sears newspapers. The story said four papers were in operation, one in the Kansas City area distributing 40,000 copies under several local datelines. "Editorially, the papers have confined themselves to local and community news, stories on Sears doings, feature items (including serials, radio and movie columns, cartoons, etc.). Accepted and printed gratis is the classified advertising department. At first any and all advertisements were put into them, but such a flood began pouring in that a new policy has been adopted whereby an advertiser has to go to a Sears store personally to have his advertisement accepted."

It was reported that in some places where store managers

proposed to undertake such a project, newspaper reaction was so strong that the Sears executives proposed an alternative of paying the publishers to insert the store paper in their own weeklies. This particular plan soon flickered out but interest has always remained high in devising ways through inserts to ride on the admittedly high readership interest of the community weekly.

The persistent belief in such a large segment of the population that selling advertising in a special publication is a good way to make money has always been mystifying to newspapermen and other professionals in the field. Yet the proliferation of clubwomen's cookbooks, memorial books and booklets, special club or association publications, and many similar forms of fund-raising activity dependent basically upon advertising revenue all testify not only to the pervasiveness of the belief but that it has some validity. And so the print media advertising shoppers in various forms are virtually certain to persist far into the future.

The Desire To Be Heard

But there's another large and incredibly varied class of would-be publishers whose interest in advertising revenue is peripheral; they hope mainly to attract enough advertising to pay all, or even a part, of their expense without really being concerned too much about a profit. Their primary concern is to be heard by a broader audience than is available in conversation with a roomful of people, or even in front of a soapbox in a park, and in a more sustained way than through letters to the editor. Surely a symptom of this yearning is to be seen in the popularity of talk shows and "open forum" programs on radio and television. Even where the volunteers know there is an excellent chance they will be needled, even insulted, by the conductors of these shows, they flock to the microphones. Yet most are undoubtedly left with an unsatisfied feeling that they may not have reached the right targets in that misty mass "out there"; that the ones in a position to "do something" may not have been listening or watching. The relative permanence of print, the possibility of "aiming" it directly at a select target audience, exercises a continuing fascination, and we find hundreds of persons making great sacrifices to publish their views in little papers of limited circulation. As the population increase and consequent urban crowding make our social problems more pressing and complex, we may expect an intensification of individual efforts to be heard, in the manner of little bubbles from a fermentation process forcing their way up through a mash.

An interesting case history of a good specimen is related by Rick Friedman, who quoted from articles by local political writers printed in the last issue of the Lowell (Mass.) *Optic*, a paper founded in 1927 as the personal organ of a man evidently deeply concerned with local and state politics. It was continued after his death in 1961 but apparently never was more than a marginal operation. Views expressed by the political writers included these comments:

I have always felt that the Lowell *Optic* served a fine purpose, and I still believe this. A newspaper diet should be more than pablum and the Lowell *Optic* has provided spice. No one has ever made pretensions that the Lowell *Optic* was a great newspaper or even, possibly, that it was a newspaper at all in the traditional sense.

. . . There are two main factors involved in understanding the influence enjoyed by the *Optic*. First, it was one of the last papers devoted exclusively to politics in the state. . . . Second, by virtue of its location in Lowell, the *Optic* has pre-eminent importance to candidates for state office. . . . The small weekly, especially one that confines itself to the perusal and explanation of politics, is probably doomed to extinction, through the spread of larger, more widely distributed mass media.

. . . Lowell needs a voice of dissent, a sometimes violent, frequently dangerous, but always vigorous voice of dissent, no matter how good the times seem, no matter how steady seems the hand on the tiller, no matter how blissful everyone else happens to be about what's happening. The *Optic* was Lowell's voice saying NO in thunder. Such a voice is worth the price it costs. And when this voice goes silent now, it's a loss for Lowell.[17]

Perhaps the *Optic* took too narrow a view of its mission. A paper which ranges widely over all sorts of social problems, the *Village Voice* of Greenwich Village in New York City, now makes a claim of being the nation's "largest community weekly"

---

[17] "The Weekly Editor," *Editor & Publisher*, January 7, 1967.

with a circulation of 54,396 (end of 1966). But to achieve such a figure it promotes itself through little bookstores and on college campuses all over the country. As *Time* magazine reported, "Few Village fancies escape the attention of the *Voice*. No Village fad—from psychedelic shopping centers to erotic Christmas ornaments—is too eccentric to be ignored." The paper was founded in 1955 by a group, including author Norman Mailer, who thought the Village needed an outlet for views and writers opposed to the Establishment. As the paper matured and grew ambitious to be heard outside of the Village, it seemed to gain in objectivity and detachment. *Time* concluded its article with "As the *Voice* goes international, it risks losing its ties to the Village and its unique New York flavor. Indeed, another paper, the *East Village Other,* has already sprung up to champion all those causes—from LSD to pansexualism—that the *Voice* views with skepticism. But the *Voice* is unworried. 'EVO is for the totally alienated,' says [Assistant Editor] Jack Newfield. 'We're the paper for the partially alienated.' "[18]

A more traditional community weekly, *The Villager,* has been serving the area since 1933, and thus apparently completes the newspaper spectrum for the diverse residents.

There have been, and continue to be, many forms of protest publications which at least resemble newspapers, even if they may not legally qualify as such, and which in isolated cases might later develop into true community weeklies, legally qualified. Some carry a tag of "underground" although nothing in this land of the free forces them underground or into any kind of clandestine existence. The term seems to be loosely used to cover newspapers with an irregular schedule and a precarious financial footing, some having to flee unpaid printing bills. We have examples of these on or near college and high school campuses; papers issued by dissident student groups who feel that the established college newspaper is too much under the thumb of the Establishment. We have had many and interesting examples of "beat" and "hippie" newspapers as these movements emerged in the mid and late sixties. To be sure, the communities such publications serve are shifting and unstable, but the papers certainly illustrate the point that when there is a strong desire to be heard, just about the first thought is to establish a newspaper.

---

[18] "Voice of the Partially Alienated," *Time,* November 11, 1966.

The desire to be heard is not always based on a wish to protest. New weeklies are being founded just because someone feels that he wants to be a newspaperman, or because he feels that the community needs a paper, or both. An example is John Henry Cutler, a Ph.D. who had been teaching romance languages at Dartmouth, and who wrote a light-hearted account of his experiences in founding the Duxbury (Mass.) *Clipper,* now a successful weekly.[19] Without previous experience, he and his wife operated the newspaper out of their home, contracted out the printing, and made the *Clipper* a success in a surprisingly short time. Although he lacked newspaper experience, Cutler had proved himself as a popular writer, and his paper succeeded because of the special flavor he could bring to its pages, much appreciated by a sophisticated audience which made Duxbury a resort town.

Or, in another case, a paper was started on a home dining room table because a housewife felt that the community of Syosset, New York, needed its own paper. Her problems were smoothed by the fact that her husband operated a good commercial printing plant in an adjacent town, but essentially all that meant was that she could get a favorable printing contract. The success of the paper resulted from a shrewd recognition that the community was ripe for the venture, a deft writing touch, and great energy. A decade after founding, the Syosset *Tribune* claimed a paid circulation of 4,500 and printed eight to sixteen tabloid pages a week.

There's Community Desire, Too

Sometimes a group rather than an individual personifies that urge for a voice in the community. The history of the Park Forest (Ill.) *Reporter* may be cited. It started in 1949 as a mimeographed publication on standard 8½ x 11 sheets, produced by a group of housewives and distributed free to 150 families living in a new development. Within two years the real estate developers had 3,100 rental units built and a village was incorporated. The original group producing the paper formed a nonprofit organization to expand and develop the *Reporter* in order to keep residents informed about their com-

---

[19] *Put It On the Front Page Please!* New York: Ives Washburn, 1960.

munity and its efforts to promote social and cultural contacts. As the village grew, the paper thrived and soon became too complex a business operation for its volunteer board. Accordingly, one of the board members purchased it in 1951 and since has developed it into a standard-size printed newspaper of 16,000 circulation (10,000 paid).

These impulses toward a voice in political or social activities; toward improved communication with a community; or toward improving its image as a commercial center show no signs of diminishing. Small radio stations, although they continue to increase in number and often are business enterprises comparable in size to weekly newspapers, do not satisfy these needs. Because they must necessarily be licensed and regulated by a federal authority in order to prevent chaos on a limited number of transmission channels, they will always lack the independence needed for a variety of voices of dissent.

Nor need it be assumed that dissent is feasible only in the relatively sheltering anonymity of the big city. Garrett W. Ray, editor and publisher of the Littleton (Colo.) *Independent,* writes that ". . . the weekly newspaper may be one of the last strongholds of Individualis Americanis—the lonely individual, seeking to find his own truth and speak his own thoughts freely and publicly. He may still find his forum as editor of a small paper in a farming community. This remains true even though the decline in rural population is forcing a corresponding decrease in the number and strength of these papers."[20]

A telling illustration of the strength of the conviction that the print medium remains the best way for the disadvantaged, or those who feel themselves to be such, is offered by the proposals made to start weekly newspapers "for the poor" as part of the Office of Economic Opportunity programs. The suggestions so far have been shouted down, but more because they envisioned rather elaborate enterprises embodying the fault which has drawn the most bitter criticism of the War on Poverty activities—the need for a large comfortably salaried staff who would be "doing something for" the poor. Beyond that, they were immediately suspect as government organs, a form of subsidized press.

Any efforts by the disadvantaged to organize newspapers on their own initiative to speak for a submerged economic

---

[20] "Suburbs Spell Opportunity," *Publishers' Auxiliary,* December 3, 1966.

group could only be welcomed, and methods of support through low-cost loans and services of expert advisory boards could be provided without any danger of government domination or partisan control. But the blunt truth is that among the disadvantaged there will rarely be found the talent, energy, and dedication which can make such an enterprise succeed without permanent subsidy (persons with the needed qualities may be "poor" temporarily, but they need not remain so). Nor is there any evidence that the classes which the War on Poverty attempts to help feel any need for or identification with publications intended solely for them. Lastly, it is difficult to see an economic base, through either circulation revenue or advertising, to enable such papers to be self-supporting.

Just as our review of the origins and development of the community press in the United States indicated a willingness on the part of editors to undergo all kinds of hardships in order to have their own newspapers, so we may expect to find the present rebellion against conformity to produce an equal (or greater) percentage of men and women in the future ready to make great sacrifices for their desire to be heard. And the way in which technical progress is reducing the hardships and minimizing the obstacles for the fainthearted is the subject of the following chapter.

Chapter 9

IMPACT OF THE NEW TECHNOLOGY

THE IMPRESSIVE NUMBER of the nation's weekly newspapers switching to offset is at least as much a symptom of the desire to be freed of the shackles imposed by some steps of the hot metal processes in letterpress as it is a move to reduce costs or to improve the appearance of pictures. In fact, no clear case can be made for any substantial reduction in costs where wage scales are comparable.

The skills required for printers in most aspects of the letterpress process take longer to acquire. Partly for historical reasons they lend themselves better to tighter union controls. In periods of high employment operators of small shops, impatient with the lack of qualified printers, turn to training their own, and any process or equipment which is less complicated is naturally welcomed. It has been frustrating to industry in general to learn that in the 1960's, while the general population rose 20 per cent, the working force increased by only 6 per cent.

Where it is possible to substitute typists for linecasting machine operators, it is obvious that a vast new labor pool is opened up. This is the one area where a quick gain is possible. In photography, platemaking, and presswork the skills required for good work by offset may be as complicated and take as long to acquire as comparable proficiency in letterpress. But if the stereotyping process can be bypassed, the role of women can be extended, and certainly offset plates can be managed much more easily than type forms in chases, or stereotype plates.

There is no point in debating here the comparative merits of letterpress *vs.* offset, or of skilled union labor *vs.* nonunion workers, or many similar aspects of the production processes. We wish only to make the point that because of simpler equipment and procedures, more nonprinters can meet all the varied demands imposed on the publishers of small papers. Manufacturers have steadily improved the capacity and reduced the prices of offset press units until a remarkable range of presses to meet the requirements of virtually every size and type of small newspaper operation is available. At the same time the versatility and suitability of the machines for type composition have opened the way for limitless experimentation with small publications. An analogy can be drawn with another mass medium, the film. *Time* magazine noted that professional-level film-making away from large, costly studios became possible only after "cameras, lights, recording equipment diminished in size, weight, and cost. Suddenly almost anybody could make movies and make them almost anywhere for almost nothing. Hundreds of men and women began to make them."[1]

The Rise of the Central Plant

The similar developments in the printing industry have also made feasible the type of operation which many well-qualified observers see not only as the weekly's hope for survival, but its assurance of an expansion in numbers, circulation, and impact. This is the centralized printing plant, either as a cooperative operated by a group of publishers or as a private contractor offering a specialized service. The former is the currently popular type among "country weeklies" and the latter serves mainly metropolitan neighborhood and suburban papers. This service is not at all a new development, of course. For decades the neighborhood papers, the foreign language press to some extent, Negro papers, and many forms of shoppers and other specialized publications have contracted to have their production work done rather than maintain their own plants.

[1] "The New Underground Films," *Time,* February 17, 1967.

Suburban weeklies naturally made good use of the inherent economies and efficiency in multiple publications from the very outset of the period of their most rapid development after World War II. As far back as 1928 Frank Parker Stockbridge wrote an article for the *Saturday Evening Post* about the changing image of the small town newspaper and observed, "Country papers are still started on shoestrings, without a printing plant at all, getting the paper printed in the nearest good-sized town."[2] We have already recorded in a previous chapter how the ready-print system of an earlier day greatly facilitated this process of "jobbing out" a newly founded weekly.

In the mid-1950's in an article examining the challenge to the weekly in the small village to move or die, this author expressed the view that the future for the rural weekly might lie in adopting the suburbans' method of centralized printing plants.[3] A consulting engineer specializing in the newspaper industry, J. W. Rockefeller, Jr., wrote to say he held the same view, and enclosed a reprint of an article he wrote, "What's the Future of Offset for Newspapers?" He discussed the new equipment then in sight for newspapers and concluded, "An investment of $100,000 will set up a central printing plant with a capacity of 20 weekly newspapers, or in the small daily field, at least a morning and evening edition. An investment of a few thousand dollars, assuming he will utilize the facilities of the central plant, will put a man in the newspaper business. Here indeed lies hope for a reversal in the decreasing trend in dailies and weeklies. Here, also, perhaps resides the promise of another era in journalism such as the late 19th century. With the entry tab marked down to a mere two or three thousand dollars, isn't it logical to suppose that everybody's going to get into the newspaper publishing act? And if just one of these $3,000 investments produces another Horace Greeley or a James Gordon Bennett, who will deny that it's the best bargain of the century?"[4]

Not all would agree that it is desirable to attract "everybody" into the weekly newspaper field. A Canadian publisher complained that centralized plants "have opened the door to every would-be newspaperman or woman in the world to come

---

[2] "Small-town Press," *Saturday Evening Post*, February 26, 1928.

[3] John Cameron Sim, "Weekly Newspapers Again Facing Challenge to Move," *Journalism Quarterly*, Spring, 1958.

[4] "What's the Future of Offset for Newspapers?" *Modern Lithography*, May, 1958.

into the confines of (an existing paper) and open up shop. What does it take today to go into the weekly newspaper business? Just a typewriter, a desk, a table smooth enough to draw a few lines on and you're in business. . . . Any smart young fellow with $500 in capital can go right into any weekly backyard and open up shop. If it doesn't go, so what. There isn't must of an investment, anyway. . . . The value of the business has decreased. The once exclusive field has diminished, leaving it open for every would-be editor in the country. Some weekly editors have bred a monster that is going to devour them. . . ."

When this view was reprinted in the bulletin of the Minnesota Newspaper Association it drew an immediate retort from John Tilton, then publisher of Twin City Suburban Newspapers, Inc., a group of twenty-four papers. He said, "In my book one exciting advantage of our business is that men *can* go in business with 'a typewriter, a desk, a table smooth enough to draw a few lines on' and, more importantly, if they're good enough they can become successful, shoving us aside in the process. What better way to keep all of us sharp than the prospect of competition? In our field we have three or four new publishing enterprises starting every year. Most of 'em last a few issues but some remain to become successful publications. What's so wrong about that? . . . Our Canadian friend looks at the wrong 'monster that is going to devour us.' The monster we have to fear is obsolescence—of both minds and machines."[5]

In 1959 Jay Thornton, publisher of the Haleyville (Ala.) *Advertiser* whose plant was then printing five weekly and two monthly publications, wrote in a letter to the author that "It has long been my belief that the central printing plant is the only avenue of survival for weekly papers. . . . The weekly newspaper industry as a whole is sick, just as are some other industries, and unless new methods and new ideas are employed, the mortality rate will roll higher."

Joint Arrangements Nothing New

Cooperative arrangements among rural weekly publishers have existed in limited forms almost from the time an area had

---

[5] The two comments from *Confidential Bulletin,* Minnesota Newspaper Assn., January 31, 1966, and February 7, 1966.

more than one newspaper. After business in the United States began to adopt discount systems for volume purchases, it was common for several publishers in a compact area to purchase their newsprint, perhaps in carload lots, to obtain the volume discounts. Stories of publishers banding together to provide facilities for a fellow publisher whose plant was destroyed by fire, flood, tornado, or other disaster, or to aid a publisher unable to produce his own paper because of illness or other distress, are commonplace. They get comment only when well-intentioned attempts backfire, as in the instance related by Mrs. Tom B. Ferguson, who carried on an Oklahoma paper after the death of her husband, a former governor of the state. She recalled an incident from one of her husband's campaigns:

The *Hardesty Herald,* away out in No-Man's-Land, was edited by Dick Quinn who had been summoned to answer a charge of libel . . . leaving a tramp printer in charge. . . . Left alone, the printer amused himself by putting in type some vulgar stories, then got drunk and deserted the shop. Dennis Flynn, who was making his first campaign for Congress, accompanied by Tom Ferguson, drove into Hardesty and called on their friend Quinn. No paper had been printed that week, and unless one came out in a few hours, the paper was in danger of losing its status as a legal publication. So it was up to Flynn and Ferguson to act as good samaritans, which they proceeded to do. They filled the forms with type set by the printer, old cuts, and standing ads, ran off the papers, and mailed them without ever having read any of the articles. . . .[6]

By 1961 a number of voices had predicted that the centralized plant had to be the answer of the future to steadily rising costs and the lack of mechanical department employees. Clyde E. Moffitt, publisher of the Fort Collins (Colo.) *Coloradoan* told an Oregon newspaper convention that he believed publishers would see "a fairly complete change in production methods on all of the daily papers, and most of the weeklies, in my time . . . and whether we altogether like the idea or not, I believe we are going to combine to survive."[7] In early 1962 a group of suburban Buffalo, New York, publishers formed a cooperative to set up a printing plant with a new four-unit offset press. But this might be considered a rather natural de-

[6] *They Carried the Torch: The Story of Oklahoma's Pioneer Newspapers* (Kansas City, Mo.: Barton Publishing Co., 1937).
[7] "Combined Printing of Small Papers Seen as Only Answer to Survival," *The American Press,* November, 1961.

velopment in a suburban area since the suburban field had a long tradition of contracting out newspapers for the production processes.

The cooperative which attracted the most attention in the "country" field, in no small part because of the later missionary zeal of one of the founders in appearing at state press association meetings to describe the operation, was that of Southern Lakes Publishing, Inc., which set up its plant at Delavan, Wisconsin. This brought together ten individually owned newspapers which retained their own composing room operations, some going to cold-type composition, others retaining for a time their hot metal operations. William E. Branen, editor of the Burlington (Wis.) *Standard-Press* and a past president of the Wisconsin Press Association, was chosen as president of the cooperative, and the figures he compiled on page costs, increases in classified advertising linage, and general circulation growth of the members were quite persuasive in leading to creation of at least a dozen other cooperatives in Wisconsin and Minnesota within the next four years.

Fear Loss of Control

The early advocates of central plants found that most rural area publishers resisted the concept because they feared a loss of their independence of action. The publisher saw himself bound to a tighter schedule than ever before while at the same time surrendering a final determination of when and how his paper might be printed. If he was asked to sign an agreement with a neighboring daily or a large weekly for his presswork, he had visions of returning at the contract expiration date to find himself confronted with a steep raise in rates and being fairly helpless because he would have disposed of his press in the meantime. If he was asked to join a cooperative, the publisher usually was concerned about a fair determination of the share of costs when one paper might grow more rapidly than another, or he worried whether cliques among other members might dominate the corporation to his disadvantage. Those who felt that their papers might lose their individuality and distinctiveness of appearance by being published in the same plant with their neighbors usually resolved such doubts by retaining complete control of the composition in their own plants. Indeed, state laws in many cases made it mandatory, or at least advisable, to limit central plant operations across county lines to just the presswork.

Experience of the early cooperatives seemed to dispel most of the fears about "getting trapped" held by small paper publishers.

The interest in central printing plants parallels the rapid development of suitable web offset press equipment, cheaper and better printing plates, and more acceptable typesetting equipment. The most persuasive argument for cooperation, of course, is that a group can more readily raise the sizeable amount of capital required for a modern printing plant and, just as important, assure an adequate volume of work to operate such a plant efficiently. Improvement of all-weather highway facilities extends the radius of the area which may be conveniently served by plants—the publisher can easily transport his plates on his page pasteups to the central plant, then later convey the printed papers back to his hometown post office for mailing or to distribution points for carriers. The travel takes time, to be sure, but the gains made possible by the much faster presses will either entirely or to a great extent compensate for travel time.

Progressive publishers have been quickly won over when they ponder the much improved quality the new, modern equipment makes possible for their newspapers. Good offset printing adds new clarity and sparkle to halftone pictures. Color not only may be offered to advertisers but used much more readily on the news-editorial side. There is greater flexibility in offering different page sizes in the same or special editions.

One of the basic complaints of national advertisers when they discuss their reasons for a decreased use of the weekly press is the poor reproduction that their carefully prepared advertisements too often get on antiquated presses or because the pressmen are ill-trained or careless. The central plant is geared to provide a better, more uniform quality of presswork.

Where some savings might have been achieved on a haphazard basis through group purchasing, the central plant can formalize and broaden the arrangements, obtain better credit facilities, and reduce the expense individual publishers would have to bear for warehousing and transportation of newsprint and other supplies. The necessary warehouse space can be planned when the cooperative builds, buys, or rents its building.

Saves Space and Time. On the other hand, each individual publisher stands to gain some working space, often badly needed, when he no longer needs his own pressroom or paper storage. There is quite a bit of evidence that the availability of this space, plus the intangible incentive from belonging to a progressive group, impels members to improve the interior and exterior of their hometown places of business.

The evidence on whether great savings in costs are achieved is at best inconclusive and at worst contradictory. Branen believes his Wisconsin group can show definite reductions in costs. In 1964 he offered figures for his own paper indicating an overall production cost of $47 per page and said he believed letterpress costs for comparable work would run $57 to $59 a page. As his group gained experience and improved its purchasing practices it was able to reduce costs involved in negative and platemaking, newsprint waste, and general overhead.

Although apparently only tentative and infrequent efforts have been made to use the cooperative organizations to advantage in selling retail display advertising, offering more attractive rates or decreasing its production costs, a big advantage has been found in the field of classified advertising. There have been instances where publishers first collaborated in the production of a group insert section for want ads, then progressed to a cooperative for printing their complete papers. Many of the heaviest users of classified linage—auto dealers, real estate agents, employers among others—appreciate the combination rates, the convenience, and the much wider coverage these multi-paper want ad sections give them.

Finally, it is logical to expect that whatever the local employment conditions or wage scales may be, there will be definite gains in controlling production costs. The inherent economies American business has found in mass production can now be applied to the small newspaper. This very fact raises a spectre for some editors—they envision conditions such as have resulted in the automobile industry. One editor at a state newspaper convention cried in alarm that if the present trends continue he foresees a day when "all the newspapers in this state will be controlled by three or four huge corporations!"

Costs should be controlled better because the central plant will find it easier to recruit and keep skilled employees, and to hone their skills to a sharper edge. If the supply of skilled workers continues to be short, the central plant is in a better position to train apprentices. The plants have better working conditions and are able to control hours more effectively—an important consideration in view of the insistent trend toward a shorter work week. The larger employee group normally has a more favorable eligibility for fringe benefits of various kinds, especially hospitalization and life insurance. Small individual newspapers rarely are able to establish effective retirement benefit programs, whereas the larger, better-financed coopera- tives at least have some potential for supplementing the Social Security checks of their retired employees.

Chance To Build Gross

The greatest benefits to the small town publisher of the centralized plant should lie not in the areas of reduced costs, but in the opportunities for greater revenues. The more time he can subtract from duties involving production, the more time he should be able to devote to better news coverage or more thoughtful editorial comment, which improve his pri- mary product and thus make it more salable. If his interests incline more toward the business side, he can devote more time to contacts with his advertising customers or to improvement of his circulation sales methods. It has always been true, of course, that most publishers under-value their own time and spend too much of their working day in activities which they could better afford to pay others to do.

It should not be imagined, however, that switching to central plant production will provide large segments of blissful free time for an editor or publisher. He will now have new obligations of meeting with the board which supervises the central plant, arranging and supervising the much increased travel between his editorial office and the plant, and pushing his staff to meet the rigid deadlines imposed by the close sched- uling which the central plant must enforce under present-day conditions which make Wednesday the most-wanted printing day for weeklies.

It is in this area of scheduling that the greatest chances for friction among members of the cooperative lie. Marion Krehbiel, widely known newspaper broker who always cautions prospective buyers about the difficulties involved in two-man partnerships, says he strongly believes that the central plant is the answer for small town newspapers, but that the biggest drawback is that a man takes on several partners instead of one. "Partnerships, like marriages, require a lot of unselfish giving and taking—the divorce is often tougher than a marital divorce."[8] The cooperative is really a corporation, not a partnership, but the small number of members involved and their equal status does give the arrangement many aspects of a partnership. Theoretically no one member can dominate, but at the same time a dissenter has little choice but to go along with the majority, hence the need for the unselfish giving and taking.

The offset presses of a central plant will ordinarily have the capacity to turn out all the copies for a dozen weeklies of various circulation sizes on a Wednesday, but it is clear that to maintain such production requires precise timing. The plates for the next newspaper must be ready when the run for a preceding paper has been completed. Most agreements provide that if a member paper misses its press period starting time, it must drop automatically to the end of the production cycle. Determination of how the starting times shall be allocated in the first place has not proved to be a serious problem, according to Branen and others who have made reports on their operations.

The peak period caused by the demand for a Thursday dateline makes it desirable for the central plant to have other work to keep the press busy on other days. This in itself has turned out to be a stimulant for the gross income of participating newspapers, because they have an added incentive to go out for commercial printing jobs in their communities which they could not have handled before either because of a lack of equipment or lack of time. The plant will not be interested in trying to build a full five- or six-day volume of work because ordinarily about a full day has to be devoted to cleanup and maintenance each week. Branen says that careful adherence to a rigid pre-

---

[8] Marlan D. Nelson, "Centralized Publishing: How It Operates, Its Pros and Cons," *The Iowa Publisher,* December, 1964.

ventive maintenance schedule really pays better than whatever profit might be derived from running the press that extra day.

Staffing has not been an especial problem for those cooperatives which have reported on their operations. The central plant has not meant layoffs or discharge for employees of the participating members; where employees could not be fitted into positions in the central plants, it has ordinarily been true that they were easily retrained for other positions in the home shop and were needed because of the increased volume of other work the paper now could handle.

Great Development Expected

It can safely be predicted that present-day central plant operations bear about the same relationship to what will develop in the future as colonial plants bear to the typical operation of today, but the changes will arrive in the accelerated fashion which marks all current technological development. As computers are made smaller and cheaper, yet even more versatile, it is easy to see the many applications they will have for a central plant. Electronic transmission systems for pasteup pages or proofs to be printed will make it possible to draw papers from a broader area into a central plant; this greater concentration of capital and credit will permit purchase of more sophisticated and automated equipment, which will in turn permit greater production—an ever-expanding cycle. Transportation of printed papers back to a home post office is no problem even with today's facilities, but transportation methods certainly will continue to improve, and it is also probable that existing laws which require mailing of newspapers in the post offices of their home communities will be changed when the need becomes insistent enough.

Federal small-business loan assistance has not been available to newspapers and radio stations in the same way it has to most forms of small enterprises, but an increasing number of private financing concerns have shown some interest in making loans to community newspapers, although not on terms as favorable as those of the Small Business Administration. If the oft-expressed sentiments of public figures about the importance of the community newspaper to the fabric of democracy are sincere, we may expect some philanthropist eventually to establish a foundation which will specialize in low-cost loans to small town newspapers, or a foundation now in existence may add this kind of activity to its present list of undertakings. This would certainly encourage development and expansion of the central plant idea as the most efficient and safest way to use the loans. Journalists generally agree that it never will be desirable to have government of any kind step into this picture, either through the Small Business Administration or any other agency, but foundation-administered loan programs would be reasonably free of suspicion of subversion or control. In any case, dangers of control by undesirable elements exist today under present circumstances, and it is difficult to see how an openly administered loan program would add measurably to any threat to a free press.

Suburban newspapers are definitely moving along with the rest of American business in the trend toward merger and consolidation. Scarcely a week goes by but that a suburban chain somewhere in the country announces acquisitions, from single small papers to sizeable groups. Here is a scattering of typical headlines for a period of a year in 1966–67:

In Philadelphia

**INGERSOLL BUYS GROUP
OF 6 WEEKLY PAPERS**
*   *   *
**HOLLISTER ADDS TWO NEWSPAPERS
TO SUBURBAN WEEKLY GROUP**
*   *   *
**GANNETT COMPANY PURCHASES
10 SUBURBAN GROUP WEEKLIES**
*   *   *

In Northern Virginia

**SUBURBAN AREA
HAS NEW WEEKLIES**
*   *   *
Now 29 Papers

**TWIN CITIES SUBURBAN
NEWSPAPER CHAINS MERGED**
*   *   *
**CHICAGO GROUP BUYS
2 CALIFORNIA PAPERS**
*   *   *
**HICKS-DEAL PUBLICATIONS BUYS
8-NEWSPAPER WAVE GROUP IN L.A.**

And a news story lead: "CHICAGO—America's largest weekly newspaper group this week announced plans for publication of two new newspapers, making the Lerner Home Newspaper total now 33 newspapers each week."[9]

A few months later a criterion of size of circulation rather than number of units was used as the leadership palm was awarded to another weekly newspaper group: "CHICAGO— The Chicago-based Economist Newspaper Group has become the largest community newspaper chain in the nation with the purchase of the San Diego *Independent* and *County Independent,* two . . . California . . . weeklies with a combined circulation of 255,000. In making the announcement, Economist Publisher Bruce Sagan indicated $1,500,000 was involved in the purchase [which] brings the number of publications in the group to 20 . . . with a total circulation of 572,000, largest of any weekly newspaper chain in the country."[10]

The purchase of weekly newspapers by dailies has been a closely watched development in the field. When the Fort Worth (Tex.) *Star-Telegram* announced in January, 1967, that it had acquired stock in its fifth suburban weekly, it said that several different advertising packages would be offered through the daily and the suburban weeklies. The Toronto (Ont.) *Telegram* indicated that when it bought five weekly newspapers in March, 1966, it believed the weeklies could offer advertisers additional impact in a rich market. Cowles Communications, Incorporated, bought three Long Island weeklies to use their circulation as a nucleus for the new daily newspaper the company founded at Deer Park, illustrating a third approach (besides the Field Enterprises and Chicago *Tribune* efforts in the Chicago area discussed on pages 71–76) that metropolitan dailies and chains may use to meet the competition offered by the suburban press. The Gannett Company statement at the time of its purchase of ten New Jersey suburban weeklies said the expansion is "part of a policy of maintaining the best public service and coverage of hometown news in a growing community. Even more than a metropolitan daily, a weekly can provide a detailed account of the news of its own neighborhood."[11]

---

[9] "Lerner Group Plans 2 More," *Publishers' Auxiliary,* June 18, 1966.
[10] "Chicago-Based Group Becomes Lead Chain," *Publishers' Auxiliary,* October 22, 1966.
[11] "Gannett Company Purchases 10 Suburban Group Weeklies," *The Jersey Publisher,* June, 1966.

Infusion of new capital in this way is just one more prop to support a belief that computer systems will be extensively applied in the weekly newspaper field, as well as the daily, within the next few years. The immense potential of even small computers makes them better fitted for group operations, and it is easy to see that computers will now make possible combinations which otherwise might have been too unwieldy or too complicated. The trend to merger and group expansion so marked in the mid-Sixties may therefore be expected to continue at an accelerated pace.

New and "Far-Out" Distribution Systems?

At present distribution problems are the most serious limiting factor in the expansion of numbers and size of suburban papers. A series of increases in second-class postage rates created problems of using the mails to serve subscribers in thinly populated suburban areas. Increases in subscription and single copy rates have generally been accepted by readers as to be expected in an inflationary period, but it is evident that competitive situations are primary considerations. The suburban weekly builds on its role as a second paper; if its price gets too high and the suburbanite feels his budget requires him to make a choice, he will be more likely to retain the metropolitan paper —this in spite of some surveys which purport to show that he "relies" most heavily on television for his world and national news.

It is the distribution problem which impels many suburban and community (neighborhood) papers to free distribution or controlled (voluntary) circulation plans. In order to put advertising rates at a level which is essential in the absence of any substantial revenue from circulation, the publisher must offer the advertisers saturation, or at least large, circulation. It becomes more efficient and therefore relatively cheaper to have carriers deliver to every household rather than to lists of customers on routes. The mails may serve just as an auxiliary system where it is impractical to use carriers.

It is not at all unlikely that a widespread unrest over an overburdened postal system (an irritation not limited to newspapers) will force some sweeping changes in the post office which will once again make the mails a preferred system for newspaper distribution. Population growth and shifts virtually guarantee that the post office must extensively modernize its methods far beyond the rather hesitant though significant steps it has been taking.

These same population changes will affect distribution problems in other ways. The great development of apartment housing in suburbia deserves more attention from economists and sociologists. The traditional picture of the suburbanite with his house and yard, with consequent deep interest in property taxes, sewers, street paving, traffic controls, and similar problems is being sharply modified by the increased number of apartment dwellers, whose basic concerns with local government may be quite different. But for newspaper distribution, the concentration of households afforded by large apartment developments is an inviting prospect. In central city areas there has even arisen the weekly newspaper produced for the residents of a single apartment complex.

The larger chains, or associated groups of newspapers, have obvious advantages in meeting complex distribution problems. Their volume will be great enough to justify investment in transportation facilities to make newspaper delivery more efficient, and to build an organization which can guarantee enough working hours and adequate rates of pay to make the circulation jobs attractive to adults as well as to schoolboys. The volume, that is, may be adjusted to spread over a full workweek and thus enable the firm to have a sufficient number of full-time employees to provide the supervision to make the most effective use of part-time workers.

Legal problems may also make changes in distribution systems more attractive. Richard Cardwell, in his role as general counsel of the Hoosier State Press Association, says that "In utilizing carriers to effectuate the distribution of their product, newspapers fling themselves into one of the most difficult and murky areas of the law."[12] He finds that the "little merchant" system is in jeopardy because as the distribution system becomes more efficient and businesslike the independent contractor relationship tends to break down into an employment relationship. The implication is that for true efficiency the newspaper might as well go all the way and recognize its carriers as regular

---

[12] "The Carrier System—More 'Chaos' Needed," *National Publisher*, January, 1965.

employees, with all the obligations for social security, unemployment compensation, overtime, and other federal or state regulations that the employment relationship involves. The alternative, Cardwell says, is "as a general rule with carriers, the more chaos the better" to emphasize the existence of a true independent contractor relationship. That choice may be a preferable one for single newspapers but it surely will not be for large groups.

In any case, the distribution problems as they now exist may be transitory. The most common predictions about the future of newspaper technology largely focus on the means of putting the product into the hands of the consumer in the speediest manner and most convenient form. No one really has been able to envision a basic change in present methods of gathering, writing, editing, and selecting the news. The changes which are forecasted all affect the *form* of handling these processes—perhaps more electronic recording of events as they happen, systems of speedy information retrieval, writing and editing through voice-recognition computer systems, and the like. The reproduction of news and comment may be drastically altered from present processes, but the basic need of some form of reproduction which will still have a recognizable similarity to the printing press is always acknowledged.

Thus the really basic change is certain to be in the way in which the news and comment is delivered. Agreement is still general that the reader of the future will want a printed record to be "consumed" at his convenience—radio and television give him news and comment by voice and eye now and it is is easily demonstrated that while this is what the consumer wants, he still wants more; he wants what the newspaper now gives him. So while delivery to the home may be in the form of facsimile or some other computer modification of a virtually instantaneous, complete, printed record of news and comment, this is really only an improvement on the present method of having a boy bring a copy of the newspaper to the front door; it is a redesigning of models, not a basic invention.

Even so, it raises a spectrum of fascinating new questions. Won't only large daily newspapers be able to afford such transmission facilities, either separately or through combinations such as the present-day Associated Press and United Press International? How can weeklies compete, in view of the facts

that the facilities will be expensive, and the price to the consumer must still be kept relatively low? These very facts, plus
inescapable political considerations, assure that the facilities
will be operated by public utilities, either those now in existence or new ones which emerge. Further, this will relieve at
least partially the fears of monopoly; indeed, it ought to assure
that small weeklies can compete on even terms with the largest
dailies in the delivery of their product to the reader's home or
office. To what extent will these interrelationships, an undoubted power to control delivery of the product, affect and
be affected by the constitutional guarantees of freedom of
speech and of the press? A whole field of political problems is
opened up. Some writers have predicted that these developments will not only slow down the present mushrooming
growth of the use of the mails, but reverse it. This, since there
will be no sharply drawn dividing point at which publications
all at once turn to some form of electronic transmission, means
that the publications which inevitably lag behind—usually the
smallest and least favorably situated—will have a more ad-
vantageous position in the mails. Given the aforementioned
political considerations, it is quite conceivable that Congress
will grant small publications special advantages just to keep
them using the mails. Unlikely? Eighty years after the invention of typesetting machines there are still hand-set newspapers.
The transition periods for the change from one form of delivery
system to another will surely be varied in numerous ways—
areas, economic levels, construction lags, political debates, and
purely human foibles. The opportunity for various forms of
newspapers to coexist will be increased rather than lessened.

Chapter 10

THE CHANGES AHEAD

By 1966 THE Wall Street Journal had evidently arrived at a company solution for the question of what shape the newspaper field of the future will take. Vermont Royster, its editor, told delegates to the Audit Bureau of Circulation convention that "There's a place for a national daily like the *Wall Street Journal,* or national weeklies like *Newsweek, Time, National Observer.* There is a place for large regional papers—possibly only one to a region—and there is a place in every community for a newspaper that does a community job that no one else can do."[1]

The late Bernard Kilgore, then the *Journal's* board chairman, spoke at a meeting of the Milwaukee professional chapter of Sigma Delta Chi and said just about the same thing, but made it more specific. He expected newspapers to settle into four main types:

1. A few giant regional morning newspapers specializing in regional, national, and international news with a minimum of features and comics, but with advertising of broad appeal, carried at high rates.
2. Improved versions of the suburban paper, strong in local coverage and adequate in national and international coverage, probably afternoon editions, with many features and much advertising at low rates.
3. Small dailies and large weeklies to serve the news and advertising interests of smaller communities, devoted almost exclusively to local events.

---

[1] Audit Bureau of Circulations, Annual Meeting, New York, October 20, 1966.

4. Specialized nationwide publications such as the *Wall Street Journal,* providing specialized subject-wide coverage rather than geographical, wide-interest coverage.[2]

There are critics with a more jaundiced view of the future of newspapers. Marshall McLuhan says, "The classified ads (and the stock market quotations) are the bedrock of the press. Should an alternative source of easy access to such diverse daily information be found, the press will fold. Radio and TV can handle the sports, news, comics and pictures. The editorial, which is the one book-feature of the newspaper, has been ignored for many years, unless put in the form of news or paid advertisement."[3]

If radio meets the criterion of "alternative source of easy access," we should very shortly be hearing a cry of "Maggie, fetch the beads!" for the wake of the newspaper. In the summer of 1966 the Federal Communications Commission granted the application of a Los Angeles firm to buy KGLA, an FM station, and use it for a one-year trial of a program format based exclusively on classified advertisements and public service announcements. Gordon McLendon, the new owner, said he planned to operate the station from 6 A.M. to 10 P.M. The FCC was quoted, in authorizing the one-year trial, to the effect that this did not mean any change in its policy of holding licensees to account for overcommercialization, but that it was acting on a section of the Federal Communications Act which authorizes a study of new uses for radio and encouragement of larger and more effective use of radio in the public interest.[4] If nothing else, newspapers could take consolation in this affirmation of a cardinal tenet in their promotional efforts—the want ad draws great readership because it performs a vital public service.

Suggestions that the electronic media will supplant the newspaper are predicated on the assumption that these media will continue to develop pretty much in the way they have in the past. The focus of this book is on the community newspaper, and it is not its purpose to extend the examination to

[2] American Newspaper Publishers Assn., *Newspaper Information Service Newsletter,* New York, January 23, 1967.

[3] *Understanding Media: The Extensions of Man* (Signet Book [2nd ed.; New York: New American Library, Inc., 1964] published originally by McGraw-Hill Book).

[4] According to "Radio Station Ends Want Ads Format," *Editor & Publisher,* August 26, 1967, the experiment was dropped after six months. A report to the FCC showed a loss of $86,000 for the six-month period.

the future of radio and television, but it is apropos to note a statement by E. William Henry, chairman of the Federal Communications Commission, that the industry should take into account the possibility that direct-broadcast satellites may eliminate "overnight" the need for *local* radio and television stations. This would surely be an exaggeration; the need might be changed, but not necessarily eliminated. Just as in this book we have considered how newspapers have had to change, and must continue to do so in the future, so we must assume that radio and television stations may alter both their programming and their clientele drastically without going out of business. Furthermore, it is easy to imagine ways in which a reorientation might throw the broadcast media into an even more directly competitive stance versus newspapers.

McLuhan and his followers base their case for sweeping changes in the culture on the assertion that a new generation has grown up, heavily exposed for the first time to the electronic media. This re-poses the eternal question of how much—and how fast—do people really change? The cynics among us will hold to the view that human nature hasn't changed basically in all of recorded history. Robert Ardrey, in his book "African Genesis," pushes the time of any substantial changes far back into prehistory, back even to man's ancestors, contending that much of our otherwise often incomprehensible behavior (especially violence) results from basic instincts acquired from dawn man.

We make our hopeful assertions that man is becoming "civilized"—but our actions continue to belie them. We shudder as we read of the cruelties inflicted on the slaves who built the pyramids, or the victims in the Roman circuses, or in the Inquisition—but we can read of 20th-century practices of equal or greater viciousness. Or, to take it from the other end, the gentle citizens who ask "What is the world coming to?" because it isn't safe to walk alone at night in the streets of any great city or even in open spaces such as New York's Central Park, forget that it was unwise to proceed without armed escort at night in the streets of ancient Rome, or medieval Constantinope, or 18th-century London or Paris—and probably in Nineveh and Tyre.

In just a generation we shall be firmly into the 21st century. In speculating on the kinds of changes to be expected by then in mass communications, and particularly community newspapers, how much allowance shall be made for changes in human nature? On the evidence to date, we need make none. It will have changed little, if any, in that time. To be sure, most of us properly believe we have made great strides in social reform, in economic justice, in adjustments for communal living. A comfortingly large proportion of mankind has proved to be capable of making great personal sacrifices for the common good; the absolute numbers of the kind, brave, unselfish, thoughtful, sympathetic persons are growing. But are these greater numbers due to some fundamental improvement in human nature in the last couple of hundred years? It is most doubtful. The answer is that there are more people—of all kinds. In this country the population doubled between 1870 and 1900, redoubled by 1950, and reached 200 million in 1967. Projections are for a jump to 300 million by the end of the 20th century. It is all too clear from studies and statistics of many kinds that the number of "bad guys" grows proportionately with the number of "good guys," and that more facilities for education, social welfare projects, and similar efforts add only a veneer which may conceal some of the worst aspects of our society in comparison with a time when less sophisticated men violated the mores more openly.

James Reston devoted one of his columns to this problem, declaring, "in fact, this question about the corruption of personal and institutional standards in America is the one thing that troubles most of the leaders on all sides in the current controversies. . . they are united on one proposition—that something is wrong, that there is now no common code of conduct in the United States that unites the nation and guides its people about what is right and wrong."[5] This is a symptom of what sociologist Daniel Boorstin in another context calls our "disease of extravagant expectations." We have wistfully expected that all our education, our wealth, our devotion to established religious forms and institutions of all kinds will cause some changes in human nature that go deeper than the surface—and we continue to be extravagantly disappointed.

Expecting Too Much of the Press

W. H. Ferry, vice president of the Fund for the Republic, in an article on "Masscomm as Guru," delivered a scathing

---

[5] February 28, 1967.

attack on present-day media of mass communications (Mass-comm) for its failure to accept its social and cultural leadership responsibilities.[6] His indictment is considered here for its application to the community weekly, even though he directed it more to large and powerful units among daily newspapers, magazines, radio, and television. Perhaps it can be taken to apply even more directly to weeklies because of the emphasis in the United States upon local control of governmental and social institutions, and the often-asserted opposition to greater concentration of power in the federal government. Ferry discusses the Watts riots and other incidents as "significant and not isolated instances of the failure of masscomm in the first task of education, to inform and clarify." He argues that its failures have the "prime consequence . . . [of] the stupefaction and brutalizing of the nation," and that to excuse itself on the grounds that the content offered is what the public demands is the worst kind of irresponsibility.

"I would moderate the severity of these remarks," he wrote, "if some motion toward improvement could be discerned. I see little or none. . . . It will be protested that I ask too much. The answer is that my demands are those made of liberal education wherever it is being conducted." Isn't that just the point? Why should Masscomm be expected to wreak a miracle in changing wrongs which after all are due mainly to basic aspects of human nature where other agencies of society have failed over a much longer span of centuries?

All the weaknesses and deficiencies of the community weekly that we have explored in preceding chapters may certainly be attributed to fundamental human shortcomings, and these defects are the same in the managers of all forms of the mass media—or of education, religion, business, industry, labor. Ferry's apparent belief that Masscomm should succeed where all else has so far failed is unrealistic at best—though there is certainly every reason for him to urge the mass media to try harder.

Whatever changes for the better we do discern turn out upon close analysis to be improvements in the environment, and here certainly the community press can achieve mightily—and may properly be accused of falling far short of its potential, inspiring and impressive as its past achievements may be. The

---

[6] "Occasional Papers" published by the Center for the Study of Democratic Institutions of the Fund for the Republic, Inc., 1966.

world resembles a space vehicle in the way it has been accelerating in its improvement of the environment (taken in a large sense and with no reference to the undoubted problems of air and water pollution, hunger, slum housing, etc.). It took uncounted centuries to progress from the Old Stone Age to the New Stone Age, then perhaps 6,000 years to move into the Bronze Age. Roughly 3,000 years passed before the Iron Age, then 2,000 before another great turning point of the Steam Age was reached. But then it took less than 150 years to reach the Electric Age, and an even shorter period passed before we entered the Atomic Age. Of course, all these so-called ages differed in various parts of the world; they overlap, and one continues on parallel course with another, but the rough chronology is adequate to illustrate the principle of rapid acceleration at work here. Thus, in the remaining years of the twentieth century, who is bold enough to predict in detail the impact new discoveries will have? Or that the hoped-for genetic improvement in mankind will not be realized in a way which Ferry seems to yearn for? We can take hope from the well-known lines of Arthur Hugh Clough's poem, "Say Not the Struggle":

> For while the tired waves vainly breaking,
>   Seem here no painful inch to gain,
> Far back, through creeks and inlets making,
>   Comes silent, flooding in, the main.

It is at the community press level that a base for a solid contribution from the media for improvement in human relationships may best be realized, because by its very nature the community paper can be closest to its readers. Eric Hoffer, that evangelist of the working man, observed that "Man became human by finishing himself. Yet his humanness is never finished and final. Man is not only an unfinished animal; he is an unfinished man. . . . The lust for power in particular has shown itself to be antihuman. . . . Power is power to dehumanize, and it is in the city that this lust finds the human material to work on. It is easier to dehumanize man in the mass than any individual man."[7]

If the community weekly is, as it has been called, the last

---

[7] "A Strategy for the War With Nature," *Saturday Review*, February 5, 1966.

stronghold of free individual expression, it bears a responsibility toward all men as individuals. The danger to it lies in the tremendous economic pressure to make it an instrument of mass expression, an organ of mass communication. But its strength must ultimately lie in its differences. All through its history the community weekly has tended to imitate the daily newspaper, and the most distressing fact has been that those papers which are least similar to dailies in appearance and content are those in the backwash, left far behind in another era of printing and journalism. As in everything else, there are distinguished exceptions to this pull toward conformity and imitation.

In the field of methods and equipment the weekly press for most of its history has been the ultimate beneficiary—if it can be called that—of a kind of "trickle down" process. As the bigger, more prosperous metropolitan dailies were forced by their growth to install new, faster, more efficient machines, they sold their displaced equipment to smaller dailies, who in turn sold their used machines to still smaller papers, and so on down to country weeklies. These became the end of the line; there was no one else to buy *their* used equipment, so they kept it. Thus we find 100-year-old presses still grinding faithfully away in country shops; occasionally we see one of the very earliest models of the Linotype still casting type slugs.

Now for the first time we find this picture clearly changing. Manufacturers are designing presses and composing machines especially for the small newspaper; the weekly can now buy new equipment instead of secondhand and often outdated machines. With this advantage there is no reason why weeklies should so slavishly follow the format and many of the practices of the metropolitan dailies. One example will suffice. As, under wartime pressures and controls, dailies narrowed their columns to less and less readable widths, weeklies with far less reason to follow these measures of economy nevertheless imitated their big city brethren. Now some dailies are switching to a wide-measure column, fifteen or sixteen picas, and we find some weeklies following suit, where they should have been leaders. They would have had far fewer mechanical problems in making such changes; they would have been better able than the dailies to counter resistance from advertisers and adjust rates. Community weeklies of the future must strive to be innovators, to carve out for themselves a distinctive role—and then fill it with distinction.

Groups Provide Strength for Innovation

It is the suburban community press that offers the greatest hope and opportunity for innovation. Of course, many examples can be cited now of creative and bold experimentation, of imaginative risk-taking in the suburban newspaper field. The clearly apparent trend toward larger and larger groups is providing the economic strength to command and retain the talent needed for innovation and the means to experiment.

A New York City corporation with massive funds to invest explored in depth in 1966 the possibilities of assembling a group of existing suburban chains into one large national corporation. Several meetings with key owners and publishers of suburban groups from various parts of the country were held, and unquestionably these approaches had been preceded by thorough studies of the field. The idea met the mixed reception which is typical of any proposal for merger or combination of smaller, highly individualistic businesses, whether the field be naphtha, noodles, or newspapers. There are always those who for reasons of imminent retirement, estate tax provisions, difficulties of financing needed expansion, and similar reasons are receptive to offers to buy their holdings if the offers are attractive enough. Then there are companies led by executives quite far from retirement age, not ready to think of estate transfer problems, engaged in a stimulating and challenging building effort who would as soon think of selling their eldest child. Others may place their reasons for refusing to sell on a more idealistic plane, declaring their opposition in principle to mergers which offer any threat, however remote, of monopoly. In any such negotiations an onlooker can never be sure how much faith to put in fierce declarations of independence or in denials that any thought of selling is entertained.

At the time of writing it was uncertain how vigorously the investors intended to pursue the project after the difficulties encountered in the exploratory moves. Doubtless they were prepared for such resistance and a period of advances and retreats may be expected. At any rate, it may safely be predicted that if this group of investors does lose interest, another group will come along. It is the prevailing current in American (and world) business.

E. B. Weiss, vice president of Doyle Dane Bernbach advertising agency and prolific commentator on marketing, has examined what he calls the knock-out battle between corporate and voluntary chains, and concludes, "In brief, concentration of control—in one form or another, through one corporate device or another, through one marketing concept or another—continues to be inevitable. This will be true in manufacturing, in wholesaling, in retailing."[8] The end result, despite the national unease exemplified in the sporadic efforts of the Department of Justice to prevent certain mergers, will be a greater concentration of business than ever before. There is little reason to expect that the community newspaper business is so unique that it can remain untouched by this fast-flowing current.

Newspaper chains and groups are not at all new in our history, of course, and the busy acquisitive efforts of Lord Thomson of Fleet in the United States show that national and international chains need not be limited to larger dailies. The fact that there are many suburban groups with sound, efficient organizations, with clusters of established papers having glittering growth potential, is undoubtedly attractive to many moneyed apostles of the dogma that highly skilled centralized business management, utilizing the most modern computers and communication devices, is the key to stable, assured profits. Surely these investors look beyond the economies which their management can assure to the sources of revenue they will be able to make flow more freely.

They are aware of the complaints of national advertisers about the difficulties of doing business with many individual newspapers and combinations of newspapers, and that these troubles have not been sufficiently minimized by the efforts of newspapers to combine on a voluntary basis to offer one-order, one-bill service. They have good reason to believe that a national group of suburban newspapers, with its selective high income, high education audience could offer a most attractive package to many types of national advertisers. Even more important, if the Weiss theory is correct and chains of one kind will be absorbing chains of other kinds, these top managers will in effect be talking to themselves when they discuss where

[8] "Trend: Corporate Chains Are Franchising Independent Retailers," *Marketing Insights*, February 13, 1967.

to place their ad budgets. They have an entry to their own offices which no media representatives can hope to match. The situation is not hypothetical; the example of a television network taking over professional sports teams is before us.

Would the to-be-expected outcry against such a concentration of power in a segment of the newspaper field have effect in preventing or long delaying formation of one or more national suburban newspaper corporations? Probably no more than the plaintive protests of certain sports fans had on the CBS purchase of the New York Yankees. The central combination would undoubtedly say that it would follow the Thomson pattern of local autonomy in the editorial control of the newspapers, although it is axiomatic that editorial policies which interfere with successful financial operation will be changed or modified, more or less openly. The corporation may explain, too, that it is publicly held, and therefore responsive to public control through its diversified stockholders. It will be able to discount charges of monopoly, because if it is successful surely similar corporations will speedily enter the field and provide a lively form of competition as well as another set of editorial voices—and the field is so vast that ample opportunity exists for a number of corporations. If the original entrant is not successful—well, that too will soothe fears of monopoly.

Because of the basically local orientation of suburban papers, it is virtually certain that any new combinations would follow the Thomson practice of retaining the local publisher wherever possible. The Thomson organization finds that most publishers, after they sell their business to Thomson, are willing to stay on as the local manager, receiving a salary. St. Clair L. McCabe, executive vice president, has been quoted as saying, "The Thomson organization doesn't want to purchase a newspaper unless it can contribute something to it. However, this does not mean that we do, or want to, attempt to run the editorial and news sides. We assume that a man's editorial position is a responsible one or he wouldn't have been a success with his paper. . . . We're not in favor of allowing an editorial vacuum to exist in a group operation. We are in favor of allowing editors to do the excellent job they have been doing for many years. There is no interference in the operation for, as I pointed out, we rather seek to advise, not dictate."[9]

---

[9] "Sale of Brush-Moore to Thomson Will Be Wrapped Up in December," *Editor & Publisher,* September 2, 1967.

Even without an effort to concentrate a number of groups under one central management through a massive infusion of outside capital, future expansion of present suburban newspaper operations will likely have country-wide ramifications. A striking agreement emerged when the author asked executives of three of the largest and most progressive of the Chicago suburban groups where they saw their future expansion taking them. All frankly said they did not at all feel constrained to add their next papers in contiguous or nearby territory, but said that if an attractive opportunity presented itself in another section of the country to buy, or even to start, papers there they would take it. They may well have been influenced by the fact that the Economist Newspaper Group of Chicago had in October of 1966 announced the purchase of two San Diego weeklies with a combined circulation of 225,000. The addition gave the Economist Group the largest circulation—572,000 for sixteen newspapers and four shoppers—of any suburban group in the country, according to Publisher Bruce Sagan. He added:

The purchase creates the first national community newspaper network and the first effort to break with traditional weekly newspaper operation where ownership is concentrated in a single state around a single metropolitan area. The cross-country concept is a reality today because of the phenomenal growth of the metropolitan weekly newspaper industry in the last twenty years which set the stage for creation of a national community newspaper network similar to those of Copley, Hearst, Scripps-Howard and others in the daily newspaper field. . . . We feel the purchase presents the Economist Group with exciting new opportunities, and caps dramatically the growth of our chain from the original purchase of our first publication in 1953 to the largest weekly newspaper group in the nation.[10]

Economic Potential Is Great

It should come as no surprise to find corporate financiers showing this interest in the suburban newspaper as an income-producing investment. Explosive growth of the suburbs is certain to continue for several decades. The Committee for Economic Development reports that more than half of all the population of the Standard Metropolitan Statistical Areas used

[10] "Chicago-Based Group Becomes Lead Chain," *Publishers' Auxiliary*, October 22, 1966.

by the Bureau of Census to measure urban trends (224 of them in 1965) now lives outside the central cities of these areas, and that it is the fringe areas which are growing most rapidly. "If the current trends continue," says the CED, "the majority of all Americans will live in suburbia before the year 2000."[11] Suburban areas are not easily categorized; they take all kinds of patterns, and differ widely in the same areas. Yet their residents are virtually all marked by a kind of restless mobility, an orientation toward consumption, demanding an array of services and facilities unheard of just a generation ago. Why wouldn't marketers be keenly concerned, and with them the financiers? And feeling the need to communicate effectively with this majority market, why wouldn't they seek more efficiency in the media, and to this end aim at forms of economic control?

All the forecasts for life in the future emphasize the dramatic changes which will take place in work habits and the the use of the individual's time. Not only will the workweek be shorter for the factory, clerical, and service employees, but it is said that the executive, managerial, and administrative class will be able to transact more of their business and perform more of their duties without leaving home, thus reducing the volume and frequency of commuting. The effect on the suburbs and the small towns can be immense, because of this more pervasive personal presence of restless, dynamic, work-oriented men in the local community, and their greater awareness of and identification with their home surroundings. This could lead to much more intensive efforts to change the environment. Not only will they be demanding easier, quicker access to a greater variety of services, but they will be looking with a more critical eye at local government, at facilities for use of leisure time, at transportation, and at the host of other problems common to all communities.

For these efforts, direct effective communication is essential, together with means to direct and solidify opinion. The suburban newspaper can easily be visualized as the most effective economical instrument even in a fantasyland era of direct contact electronic devices (wrist television? individual instant two-way communication?). John Diebold, a consultant who

---

[11] Research & Policy Committee of the Committee for Economic Development, "Guiding Metropolitan Growth," New York, August, 1960.

speaks and writes frequently about the world of the future and is credited by some with coining the term "automation," says the one salient fact about information technology is that it is going to produce enormous social change. As the quality of life and the rate of learning, information, travel, and communications all change, he adds, we will see a major change in living patterns, in hopes, and desires. A complete new environment will exist.

Those who take the more conservative view, and say that while marked change is inevitable it will come more slowly than the automation enthusiasts predict, have the long history of the human inclination to leave things as they are as a solid support for their view. Business has long used sophisticated bookkeeping and office machines, but how many small businessmen still add up long columns of figures using pencil and paper, and write out their monthly statements in longhand? In our own industry the linotype was put into commercial use in 1886, yet today there are isolated examples of hand-set newspapers. Almost every talk on the marvels which are to be commonplace in a few years has inserted in it someplace the clincher, "Indeed, the technology to produce it already exists," which by implication confirms the point that it is public unwillingness to forego some other pleasure or comfort which delays development of the glamorous new system or device. For instance, General David Sarnoff, chairman of the board of RCA, predicted that in the future, electronics will develop processes making it possible to go from final copy and illustrations to printing in one integrated electronic process. One result will be that newspapers, in the foreseeable future, will no longer be printed in a single location. Instead, they will be transmitted through computers in complete page form to regional electronic printing centers that will turn out special editions for the areas they govern. Local news and advertising will be inserted on the spot. Eventually, Sarnoff concludes, the newspaper can be reproduced in the home through a small copying device functioning as part of a home communications center.

Essentially all this is possible, even done to some extent, today, so the basic question remains that of how soon the general public can be persuaded to make the choice which will make the facilities practical. The cynic will contend that mass man, now evidently quite content to watch football on television, with a six-pack handy in the kitchen refrigerator, will continue to opt for this choice or similar pursuits rather than invest in a "home communications center." Obviously many will, as many now choose stereo systems, opera tickets, good books, but how soon is this likely to offer the mass market the advertiser will continue to crave?

Nevertheless, whatever the pace may be, nothing is more certain than the drastic changes ahead, barring a world cataclysm in which case the changes will still be drastic but of another kind, and that newspapers will change greatly, too. It is easy to see the direction of innovations in printing and distribution; it is not so clear how the responsibilities of news collecting, evaluation, and presentation will be affected. Further refinement and broader adoption of the devices for recording statements, interviews, or meetings, for instant communication between a reporter and his editor at the office, or for extending the range of a newsman's activity can be expected. All of these aids place greater demands on a reporter's judgment and skill, and this in turn can force changes in the way the editorial employee is recruited, trained, and compensated.

The assumption here is that the changes will come sooner and be more marked in the suburban press, but the signs are plentiful even now of the great changes ahead in the non-suburban (or country) weekly newspapers. For better or worse the field is being modified sharply, as the statistics on population shifts disclose. It is true that here the resistance to change will continue to be the most persistent and that outmoded and inefficient processes will continue in use for a surprisingly long time, even as is the case today. But the opportunities for the *kind* of weekly newspaper strongly resembling the better publications of today, though much changed and to some degree re-oriented, may not only continue to exist but be expanded.

Communities of the Future

The very same movement of population that has been creating unparalleled opportunities for suburban newspapers has been intensifying pressures which many feel are now intolerable. These critics are turning ever more attention to ways of improving the smaller community in the hope that (1) they will retain more of the young, vigorous, educated persons, and (2) attract back more of the affluent who have moved to metropolitan areas. Thus they will not only improve conditions of American society generally but reduce the crowding which is responsible for many of the ills of the metropolis.

There are those who seem to feel that it is hopeless to seek significant modifications and improvements in existing middle-sized cities, at least until better ways of inspiring and motivating citizens are found. One of their suggestions for igniting enthusiasm for remaking of a city is to provide an inspirational example of what a city *could* be; hence the proposals for "new towns" or an "experimental city."

Wolf Von Eckhardt, architecture critic for the Washington *Post,* compared the limited and modest proposals in a message to Congress by President Lyndon Johnson for low-cost, federally insured loans for new town development to the successes of the British New Towns Act of 1946, and criticized mayors of big cities for pressuring Congress into deferring action on the President's suggestions. He acknowledged that private developers have made progress on their own in carrying out a form of the "new town" concept, and examined the efforts in such communities as Reston in Virginia, Columbia in Maryland, on Catalina Island, and at Mountain Park in California. But these efforts he obviously found too limited and sporadic, and he suggested a comprehensive government program to "encourage and assist the creation of balanced communities for all kinds of people." He explained:

Not everyone will want to live in them, of course. But if we were to build just 350 new towns of 100,000 inhabitants each, they would house 35 million people, or about half of the estimated twenty-year population increase. . . . The 350 new towns would consume only a total of 3.5 million acres. . . . It is in our power to conserve seven million acres of countryside for better health and greater enjoyment not only of the new-town residents but of all our people in the metropolitan areas.[12]

Six months later John Fischer, then editor of *Harper's,* endorsed the new towns proposal as part of a more comprehensive effort to solve lingering farm problems, together with

---

[12] "The Case for Building 350 New Towns," *Harper's,* December, 1965. Later press reports indicated that in 1967 plans for Reston had to be extensively modified in order to fit available financing.

the potential hazards of unemployment caused by automation. He said the flight from the rural areas into the cities is causing problems—overcrowded schools, spreading slums, crime, race riots, rising relief costs—insoluble under the present system. He asserted it should be "entirely practical for us to design a new kind of landscape, spreading our population much more evenly throughout the nation and providing for many more people in the combined advantages of city and country life."[13]

Then in November, 1966, the University of Minnesota was granted $248,000 from the funds available for a federal planning study to produce a proposal for an experimental city, preferably to be built about 100 miles from any existing metropolitan center. Dr. Athelstan Spilhaus, former dean of the university's Institute of Technology and a long-time proponent of the new city plan, was designated to direct the study. He is enthusiastic over the opportunity to utilize present technology, and techniques he believes will be developed within a few years, to design from its beginning, for perhaps 250,000 inhabitants, Experimental City, which would never have slums, ghettos or blighted areas, which could limit traffic congestion and noise, eliminate pollution of air and water, and provide all the demanded cultural and entertainment facilities. He says old cities cannot be renewed because their haphazard collections of sewer and water lines, narrow streets, poor transit systems, utility lines, and industrial areas all work in opposition to each other rather than being integrated into a rational whole. While ideally it might be desirable to have the Experimental City self-sufficient even to the point of producing all its own food and fiber in vast greenhouses, it might be more practical to import many raw materials for food and industry.

Of what significance is all this "new city" ferment to community newspapers? The Spilhaus plan would provide "an information, communications and control facility, fully computerized and connected by multi-purpose links with every home, office, and factory to serve every need from television to grocery shopping to scientific data processing to commercial banking—even to voting."[14] This doesn't seem to leave any

---

[13] "A Possibly Practical Utopia," *Harper's*, July, 1966.
[14] From series of articles for World Book Encyclopedia Science Service, Inc., reprinted in Minneapolis *Tribune*, January 22–27, 1967. Dr. Spilhaus left the University of Minnesota in 1967 to become president of Franklin Institute, Philadelphia.

room for the conventional newspaper except as it may be one of the "raw materials" imported from the outside. But surely the inhabitants would cry "brainwashing!" if they were cut off from the usual flow of books, magazines, newspapers, television and radio, and other media of the future as a part of their planned community existence. The computerized central facility may indeed make practical on a cost basis an in-the-home facsimile news and information operation which would replace the conventional newspaper as we know it, although perhaps not alter unrecognizably the present process of gathering and processing news and comment.

Other new-town planners and many who have commented on these developments have stressed the idea of neighborhood, which would seem to offer the ideal spawning ground for the kind of weekly newspaper with which we are now familiar. Reston, Virginia, for instance, was to be based on a concept of neighborhoods each with 10,000 inhabitants, and the town composed of seven villages (thus an optimum population of 70 to 75,000).

Jane Jacobs, author of *Death and Life of Great American Cities* (Random House, 1961), makes a convincing case for the proposition that some big urban developments have quickly metamorphosed into glittering, crime-ridden, refuse-strewn slums because they were originally too sterile. They lacked the amenities of the old urban neighborhood with its little stores and taverns with apartments and little offices above where people sat on the steps, exchanged greetings, and policed themselves because they knew each other, and helped those who were in trouble or danger. Von Eckhardt makes the point that the British have learned to make their new towns more compact, to build two- and three-story town houses ingeniously stacked on hills, and "designed into this cluster are the suddenly rediscovered delights of corner stores, taverns, and other amenities, the surprising vistas, the charm, variety, and bustle that recently made places like Georgetown in Washington, D.C., Beacon Hill in Boston, or Greenwich Village in New York so popular."[15]

Doesn't that sound like an explanation why neighborhood weeklies in metropolitan center cities continue to thrive, as in Greenwich Village or in many sections of Chicago or Philadel-

---

[15] "The Case for Building 350 New Towns."

phia? Doesn't that sound like the reasons advanced for the vitality of the weekly newspaper in any small town which may be richly served by all the media of a nearby big city?

Fischer is not so glum as some of the others in viewing the prospect of rehabilitation as hopeless; he would not insist that the only way to establish a successful "new town" is to start from scratch. A Reston or a Columbia, Maryland, can still be used as a model, and in addition to such communities "others might use as a nucleus one of the existing, but dying, villages which can be found in the rural areas everywhere; they have traditions, histories, and even some buildings which ought not to go to waste."[16]

Even Spilhaus recognizes that many will fear his Experimental City as "an attempt to build some manipulated social order." Not so, he contends; he would like to see the citizen be master of his own living space, and this seems to imply the kind of facility for communication and information, the open forum for opinion, which is provided by the community newspaper. Similarly, he seems to recognize the concept of neighborhood, for in the new city there would be banks, shops, hot dog stands, theaters, and every other need, comfort, or convenience of city life.

It is axiomatic that you do not automatically assure happiness for people by doing more and more for them. There are many doubters that enough people could be persuaded to move into planned communities of the type proposed, even if many of the suggested "amenities" are carefully provided. Ervin Galantay, in the architecture column he writes for *The Nation,* reported a conversation with a builder who was considering handling one of the developments offered to assure some diversity and variety in Reston. You can't build more than one such place around here, the developer told Galantay. The founder of Reston, the builder added, has captured the "entire screwball market."

Still, the new-town concept promises to be an important, even an explosive, development on the American scene. Richard Atcheson in *Holiday* (February, 1966) reported that there are more than twenty new-town projects in various stages of planning and development in the United States "at this moment,

---

[16] "A Possibly Practical Utopia."

but so far Reston is the only one you can see and touch." The emphasis on "neighborhoods" and "villages" within the new city seems to offer a better hope that such a city will have a couple, conceivably even six or seven, weekly newspapers, dwelling exclusively on local concerns and fostering a sense of identification for the residents of a village, rather than a daily serving the entire city. The inhabitants' needs for world and national news probably can better be met by the nearby metropolitan dailies, the news magazines, big radio and television. It is probable, however, that there will be experiments with a daily offering some form of zoned circulation and special sections or pages in an effort to make one newspaper serve all the villages of the city. Trial and error seems to be the only way the pattern can finally be determined—and then it may turn out that several patterns are workable.

At any rate, however the new-town concept progresses, the maximum number even suggested by anyone to date has been the 350 offered as a sort of utopian goal by Von Eckhardt. This is a trivial number compared to the many thousands of municipalities of all sizes now existing in the United States. The question is how many of them might be suitable for use as the "nucleus" of new-town development as suggested by Fischer and how many will follow other suggested patterns in a period of rapid population growth. The basic problem of each of these units is to manage its affairs in such a way as to make the environment livable and attractive for the inhabitants and prospective inhabitants. Surely this, too, has been a historic concern of the community newspaper. More and more the local communities appear to be losing ground in their management efforts, yet their efforts cost more and more. Popular discontent with both quantity and quality of services rendered by the nation's 80,000 separate local governments is greater than it was ten years ago, when it was greater than it was twenty years before that, and fifty years before that, says the Committee for Economic Development. The CED believes that, broadly speaking, the difficulties result from the existence of so many overlapping layers of government, the fact that few of these units are large enough in population, area, or taxable resources to apply modern methods, that popular control of so many offices is ineffective or sporadic, that policymaking mechanisms are weak, the administrative organizations are antiquated, and much of the personnel unqualified (other than that, everything is dandy).

Areas Where Weeklies Could Lead

This is a catalog of defects for which we might expect community newspapers to provide the most active leadership in seeking corrective measures, but the sad fact is that not only do most weeklies default that leadership, but many actively oppose progressive efforts led by others.

Some editors in fact fear proposals to reduce the number of layers of government because these units provide a news grist which community newspapers are uniquely able to cover in breadth and depth, and because they are a source of revenue through public notice (their council and board proceedings, financial statements, bid notices, etc.) and commercial printing.

The Research and Policy Committee of the CED issued one of its Statements on National Policy in July, 1966, titled "Modernizing Local Government." The statement pointed out that approximately half of the 17,996 municipalities in the United States have fewer than 1,000 residents, and many of these are declining in population. Their decline places progressively heavier financial burdens on remaining residents if they are to maintain quality of services, and thus compounds their problems. The report therefore recommends (although several committeemen dissented on grounds that the recommendations are premature, too generalized, or too sweeping):

Most—if not all—of the 11,000 non-metropolitan villages with fewer than 2,500 residents should disincorporate to permit strong county governments to administer their services on a special assessment basis, or they should contract with counties for such services.

. . . the 2,700 counties outside metropolitan areas be consolidated into no more than 500 strong and effective units—using such criteria as minimum population, accessibility to the county seat, trading and communications patterns, revenue base, and geography.

Townships not suited to full municipal incorporation should be abolished, and their functions assumed by newly consolidated county governments.

The consolidation of school districts should be continued until every unified school system has at least 1,500 students.

When the author discusses these proposals with weekly newspaper editors the initial reaction is invariably one of resistance, even horror. Frequently the thought of such consolidation is equated with destruction of the newspaper, so strong is the identification of a weekly newspaper with a specific incorporated place. Yet strong arguments can be marshaled to support a view that a widespread program of "disincorporation" and consolidation can be the salvation of the small community weekly:

(1) The greatest weakness of most small newspapers is the constriction of their field, their base of support. They are identified with a single community; if that village is small, with a declining retail section, the newspaper is doomed, however prosperous the region may be. A newspaper may strive to "serve" nearby villages, but these rarely feel the loyalty or sense of identification with the newspaper that may mark the home community; on the other hand, the villages may feel they are economic rivals. Perceptive suburban editors have commented that a basic reason for adding editions, or starting new papers, is that residents of one community have little interest in, and may even resent, news of their neighbor, even when they adjoin, and a stranger cannot tell where one town ends and the other begins. Disincorporation would provide a more generalized community of interest with which the newspaper could identify and thus more effectively extend its field.

(2) The rapidly spreading centralized plant concept fits more neatly into a pattern of larger, stronger counties achieved through consolidation of small competing governmental units. It is already a step toward blurring that strong feeling of identification of the newspaper with a single community (true even of papers without competition in their own present counties) while at the same time it provides production facilities which enable a newspaper to serve a broadened area more efficiently. Just as governmental unit consolidation does not mean there will be a reduction or redistribution of population, so these changes need not mean necessarily a reduction in the *number* of newspapers as much as it may mean restructuring of the field each serves.

(3) There would not be any lesser amount of news of significance because of a reduction in the number of governmental units, although many of the trivial personalized items about officials might be eliminated. The newspapers would be able

to cover the significant stories with greater clarity and in detail, which most observers agree is the formula weeklies must follow if they are to survive. Each newspaper will still have its specific and limited, though larger, area to cover, and the news must still be angled to interest the audience within that area.

(4) Though many counties, under the idealized situation proposed, might be five or six times larger, the old commonality of interests, or geographical factors, or economic considerations would certainly assure that the county would be divided, formally or informally, into a number of districts for carrying out what are now largely municipal functions. In effect what had formerly been separate villages would now become the neighborhoods of a larger village, and in that sense strongly resemble the concept being developed in the new towns of Reston and Columbia. Presumably merchants in such a district would have more of a feeling of togetherness in the sense that a Chamber of Commerce encourages concerted action, they would be larger and stronger individually, perhaps more progressive, and therefore better advertisers. Competition from other media would be intensified too, but the relative conditions of competition would remain about the same.

(5) There would not necessarily be a loss in revenue from public notice, and there might well be more because it will be possible to broaden and improve the scope of public services offered. Because the larger unit will be better able to finance such expenditures, there could be less of the penny-pinching economy now applied by many small councils and boards to public notices under their control. The very theory of public notice can be better justified under conditions in which newspapers serve larger areas of common interest.

(6) It is conceivable that larger, less fragmented municipal areas (as distinguished from large municipalities) will restore the type of newspaper competition which has virtually disappeared in rural America (and is little stronger in metropolitan or suburban areas). The enlarged municipal-type district might well have the economic viability to support two or more newspapers with differing approaches and points of view. Their competition for news and advertising could well make each a better and stronger paper, though it must be admitted that on the American scene such situations have not long endured. It has been like a tug of war; once one side gains an advantage and

starts moving the other, complete victory comes in a rush and the opponents go down in disorder. Yet a cycle effect could very well operate under the new conditions envisioned here; once a newspaper is triumphant over the competition and either absorbs it or drives it out, the seeds are inevitably planted for a new contender. We have seen how the new technology promises to make such new contenders more and more feasible.

It must be remembered that while proposals for extensive consolidation seem visionary now, they must be considered in the context of a national population growing from a present level of about 200 million to 300 million by the end of the century. The pressures on the management of our society created by the sheer larger numbers of people will be intensified by the complications introduced by the glittering new technology promised us. It is difficult to think of a major invention which has really over the long run simplified our lives. Made them more interesting, more comfortable, more productive, yes. But simplified, no. Nor will the computer, the space ship, and all their kin.

Resistance Is Inevitable

Nevertheless, no one expects proposals for massive local government reorganization to meet swift and easy acceptance. The researchers admit that adoption of these recommendations —in whole or in major part—will face stern resistance. Concerted, persistent, and determined efforts by dedicated community leadership are necessary before modern and efficient local government based upon the needs of today and the decades immediately ahead can be attained.

This is the kind of leadership which community newspapers historically have been expected to provide, but as noted earlier the recommendations rub against the grain of editors who for generations have stood for local control, for election rather than appointment of many types of administrative officials, short terms for policymakers, and special boards or districts to handle newly developing problems.

The anomalous position editors sometimes find themselves in is well illustrated by the case of a daily newspaper which has consistently urged that its city council and its state legislature be reduced in size, that a number of major state constitutional officers (treasurer, auditor, etc.) be made appointive rather than elective, and that ballots generally be shortened wherever possible. Yet in an article justifiably criticizing efforts to handle metropolitan efforts through a number of special districts rather than with a unified multi-purpose agency, one of the editorial staff members based his main point not on the vulnerable weakness of proliferation and fragmentation in levels of local government, but on *lack of voter control.* The writer's intentions were good; he intended to oppose the multiplication of special districts, but he is irresistibly drawn into using as an argument the shibboleth of a lack of voter control, without making it clear that what he really advocates is a small elective body at the top exercising only a legislative, not an executive, function.

This innate feeling for as many levels of local government as are necessary to bring control down as close as possible to the individual voter is reflected in what one Washington columnist calls "a kind of liberal heresy." He quotes a high federal official as saying, "Modern liberals recognize that it is just as wrong for the federal government to attempt to do too much as to do too little. Most of our problems are best challenged where they arise, at the local level. . . . That means programs, policies and projects locally developed and locally administered— but in the context of a broader pattern that includes state and regional development, backed and supported by federal assistance and resources."

Editors who have long extolled the merits of rural independence from the metropolis, who have inveighed against "big government" and "big labor," do not find it easy to switch around to leadership of efforts to reduce the number of local government units. Yet the changing economics of the small newspaper business and of their rural areas indicate that such a change of course could be in their own best interest.

From the foregoing we draw two conclusions. One is that changes in our social and political structures will lag, as usual, well behind technological changes, and this will assure the persistence of a type of community newspaper which even now has some of the aspects of an anachronism. The other is that as the inevitable progress *is* made, the patterns indicated for the future offer the kind of matrix in which a refined, much altered but still readily recognizable type of community newspaper can flourish.

Challenge From CATV

It is surprising, in a way, that so little concern has been expressed by weekly newspapers in the past few years over the rapid spread of Community Antenna Television (CATV). In 1967 there were between 1,700 and 2,000 CATV systems (accurate figures are apparently hard to come by) concentrated in the small towns and cities where small newspapers also have their habitat. Whatever concern and controversy have been aroused by the rapid development of CATV has been largely concentrated in the television industry, and publishers have paid little heed to the CATV potential as a dispenser of news or, closer to the nerve, as a sharer in the local advertising dollar. It does not compare to the alarm felt by newspapermen in the early days of radio, yet the potential threat of CATV could be much more serious.

Up to this point the systems have done little with news beyond presenting the available network shows. A few systems have programmed, even up to the full 168 hours a week, the kind of information described by Albert Warren, editor of *Television Digest:* "Working with the AP and UPI, CATV equipment makers are producing machines that enable home viewers to read news tickers on their TV screens, getting their news as fast as newspapers and radio stations do. With its luxury of channel space in its cables, CATV can devote a full six megacycles to a news ticker. It would be prohibitively wasteful of the radio spectrum to do this over the air."[17] In other words, the TV set owner in such a system can, at any hour of the day or night, switch to the appropriate channel and read the news currently coming off the teletype.

The limitations of that for the news-hungry citizen, though, are obvious. It is something (at this stage, at least) he might glance at occasionally out of idle curiosity, the same sort of fascination that stops a passerby on the street to look in a newspaper or radio station window at a clattering teletype, but he seldom if ever feels that his news needs for the day are thereby fulfilled.

Futhermore, news wire time is always pressed just to send the national and international news budgets, so that the small

[17] "The Coming Cable TV War," *Saturday Review,* June 11, 1966. In June, 1968, two United States Supreme Court decisions appeared to open the way for a great expansion of CATV.

newspaper's supremacy in the area of local news in depth would be most difficult to challenge. It would be the rare CATV system which would want to set up the news gathering organization necessary for any meaningful presentation of local news.

Still, as Warren points out, "What's to stop CATV from providing many services other than TV? Facsimile newspapers? Shopping from the home? Library references? . . . Once you get that wideband cable into the house, once you get TV to pay the initial freight of getting it there—the door is wide open."

Thus it could become just one more form of environmental pressure to threaten the survival of that uniquely American species—the community weekly newspaper. Will the weekly adapt, or will it follow the passenger pigeon to extinction? To survive it could do no better than to follow the prescription offered by Ralph W. Keller when he was manager of the Minnesota Editorial Association. He closed his report at the 1946 MEA convention:

When the newspapers teach and practice the tolerant, unselfish, generous, forward-looking brotherhood that in less than half a century we've fought and won three wars for—

When our columns are successful not only in opening pocketbooks to buy products, but in opening minds to accept ideas—

When we encourage and induce people everywhere to read understandingly—

When the press reaches its full stature in helping to produce bountifully and distribute freely—

When we do our full share in providing for the health, comfort, and security of mankind—

When we meet these challenges by practicing, printing, and disseminating high ideals, broad vision, tolerance—

By revealing the opportunities and stimulating the ambition of our readers—

By providing truthful, interesting, informative messages on products and producers, on governments and peoples, on life and its privileges and obligations—

By keeping aflame the torch of democracy and free enterprise—

Then we are indeed building an influential, profitable, incorruptible, enduring free press.[18]

[18] Minnesota Editorial Association (now Minnesota Newspaper Association) Convention, February, 1946.

BIBLIOGRAPHY

Acheson, Sam. *35,000 Days in Texas: A History of the Dallas News and Its Forbears.* New York: Macmillan Co., 1938.

Agger, Robert E., Goldrich, Daniel, and Swanson, Bert E. *The Rulers and the Ruled: Political Power and Impotence in American Communities.* New York: John Wiley & Sons, 1964.

Allen, Charles L. *Country Journalism.* New York: T. Nelson & Sons, 1928.

————. *Free Circulation.* (No. 1 of Journalism Monographs) Baton Rouge: Louisiana State University Press, 1940.

Allsopp, Fred W. *History of the Arkansas Press for a Hundred Years and More.* Little Rock: Parke-Harper Publishing Co., 1922.

————. *Little Adventures in Newspaperdom.* Little Rock: Arkansas Writer Publishing Co., 1922.

Alter, J. Cecil. *Early Utah Journalism.* Salt Lake City: Utah State Historical Society, 1938.

Ashton, Wendell. *Voice in the West: Biography of a Pioneer Newspaper.* New York: Duell, Sloan & Pierce, 1950.

Atwood, Millard V. *The Country Newspaper.* Chicago: A. C. McClurg & Co., 1923.

Bankson, Russell A. *The Klondike Nugget.* Caldwell, Idaho: The Caxton Printers, Ltd., 1935.

Barnhart, Thomas F. "The History of the Minnesota Editorial Association 1867–1897." Unpublished Master's thesis, University of Minnesota, 1937.

————. *Weekly Newspaper Management.* New York: Appleton-Century-Crofts, 1952.

————. *Weekly Newspaper Writing and Editing.* New York: The Dryden Press, Inc., 1949.

Barry, Richard. *Father and His Town.* Boston: Houghton Mifflin Co., 1941.

Beebe, Lucius. *Comstock Commotion: The Story of the Territorial Enterprise.* Palo Alto: Stanford University Press, 1954.

Berelson, Bernard (ed.). *The Behavioral Sciences Today,* Chs. 7, 8, 11, 15, 17, 20. (Harper Torchbooks) New York: Harper & Row, 1964.

Berthel, Mary Wheelhouse. *Horns of Thunder: The Life and Times of James M. Goodhue.* St. Paul: Minnesota Historical Society, 1948.

Billington, Ray Allen (ed.). *Frontier and Section: Selected Essays of Frederick Jackson Turner.* (Spectrum Books) Englewood Cliffs: Prentice-Hall, Inc., 1961.

Bing, Phil C. *The Country Weekly.* New York: D. Appleton & Co., 1917.

Bolles, Joshua K. *Father Was an Editor.* New York: W. W. Norton Co., 1940.

Boorstin, Daniel J. *The Image: A Guide to Pseudo-Events in America.* (Colophon Books) New York: Harper & Row, 1964.

Brockway, Beman. *Fifty Years in Journalism.* Watertown, N.Y.: Daily Times Printing and Publishing House, 1891.

Brown, Buford Otis. *Problems of Newspaper Publishing.* New York: Harper & Bros., 1929.

Bruce, John. *Gaudy Century: The Story of San Francisco's Hundred Years of Robust Journalism.* New York: Random House, 1948.

Buck, Solon J. *The Granger Movement.* Cambridge, Harvard University Press, 1913.

Bush, Chilton R. (ed.). *News Research for Better Newspapers,* Vol. I. New York: American Newspaper Publishers Assn., 1966.

Byerly, Kenneth. *Community Journalism.* Philadelphia: Chilton Co., 1961.

Byxbee, O. F. *Establishing a Newspaper.* Chicago: The Inland Printer Co., 1901.

Callahan, James D. (ed.). *Jayhawk Editor—From Recollections, Writings, and Papers of A. Q. Miller, Sr.* Los Angeles: Sterling Press, 1955.

Carter, Hodding. *Where Main Street Meets the River.* New York: Rinehart & Co., Inc., 1952.

Chapin, Earl V. *Long Wednesdays.* New York: Abelard Press, 1953.

Clark, Thomas D. *The Southern Country Editor.* New York: Bobbs-Merrill Co., 1948.

————. *The Rural Press and the New South.* Baton Rouge: Louisiana State University Press, 1948.

Clune, Henry W. *Main Street Beat.* New York: W. W. Norton & Co., 1947.

Cole, Cyrenus. *I Remember, I Remember.* Iowa City: State Historical Society of Iowa, 1936.

Committee for Economic Development. *Modernizing Local Government.* New York: 1966.

Connelly, William E. (ed.). *History of Kansas Newspapers*. Topeka: Kansas State Historical Society, 1916.

Cossé, Margaret V. *The Suburban Weekly*. New York: Columbia University Press, 1928.

Cutler, John Henry. *Put It on the Front Page, Please!* New York: Ives Washburn, Inc., 1960.

Dixon, J. M. *The Valley and the Shadow; Comprising the Experiences of a Blind Ex-Editor*. New York: Russell Bros., Publishers, 1868.

Dobriner, William M. *Class in Suburbia*. Englewood Cliffs: Prentice-Hall, Inc., 1963.

————. (ed.). *The Suburban Community*. New York: G. P. Putnam's Sons, 1958.

Doll, Louis W. *A History of the Newspapers of Ann Arbor, 1829–1920*. Detroit: Wayne State University Press, 1959.

Dyar, Ralph E. *News for an Empire*. Caldwell, Idaho: The Caxton Printers, Ltd., 1952.

East, P. D. *The Magnolia Jungle; the Life, Times, and Education of a Southern Editor*. New York: Simon & Schuster, 1960.

Emery, Edwin. *The Press in America: An Interpretative History of Journalism*. New York: Prentice-Hall, Inc., 1962.

Fay, Bernard. *Notes on the American Press at the End of the Eighteenth Century*. New York: The Grolier Club, 1927.

Ferguson, Mrs. Tom B. *They Carried the Torch: The Story of Oklahoma's Pioneer Newspapers*. Kansas City, Mo.: Burton Publishing Co., 1937.

Ford, Edwin H. *Southern Minnesota Pioneer Journalism*. St. Paul: Minnesota Historical Society, 1946.

Fortune Magazine, Editors. *America in the Sixties: The Economy and the Society*. New York: Harper & Bros., 1960.

————. *U.S.A., the Permanent Revolution*. New York: Prentice-Hall, 1951.

Gallaher, Art. *Plainville Fifteen Years Later*. New York: Columbia University Press, 1961.

Gill, John. *Tide Without Turning: Elijah P. Lovejoy and Freedom of the Press*. Boston: Beacon Press, 1958.

Gotterer, Malcom H. *Profitable Small Plant Management*. New York: Conover-Nast Publications, Inc., 1954.

Graham, J. B. *Handset Reminiscences*. Salt Lake City: Century Printing Co., 1915.

Graham, Saxon. *American Culture*. New York: Harper & Bros., 1957.

Griffin, Joseph. *History of the Press of Maine*. Brunswick, Me.: J. Griffin Press, 1872.

Griffith, Louis T., and Talmadge, John E. *Georgia Journalism, 1763–1950*. Athens: University of Georgia Press, 1951.

Hamilton, Milton W. *The Country Printer, New York State, 1783–1830*. New York: Columbia University Press, 1936.

Harris, Emerson P., and Hooke, Florence Harris. *The Community Newspaper*. New York: D. Appleton & Co., 1923.

Hayes, Wayland J. *The Small Community Looks Ahead.* New York: Harcourt, Brace & Co., 1947.

Henry, R. H. *Editors I Have Known Since the Civil War.* New Orleans: E. S. Upton Printing Co., 1922.

Herrick, John P. *Founding a Country Newspaper Fifty Years Ago.* Olean, N.Y.: Privately printed, 1938.

Hicks, John D. *The Populist Revolt.* Minneapolis: University of Minnesota Press, 1931.

Hill, A. F. *Secrets of the Sanctum: An Inside View of an Editor's Life.* Philadelphia: Claxton, Remson, and Haffelfinger, 1875.

Hooper, Osman Castle. *History of Ohio Journalism, 1793–1933.* Columbus: The Spahr & Glenn Co., 1933.

Hough, Henry Beetle. *Country Editor.* New York: Doubleday, Doran & Co., 1940.

————. *Once More the Thunderer.* New York: Ives Washburn, Inc., 1950.

Howe, E. W. *Plain People.* Binghamton, N.Y.: Vail-Ballou Press, 1929.

Howells, William Dean. "The Country Printer." Reprinted for private distribution by the Plimpton Press, Norwood, Mass., with permission of Harper & Bros. 1896.

Howey, Walter. *Fighting Editors.* Philadelphia: David McKay Co., 1946.

Hudson, Frederic. *Journalism in the United States From 1690 to 1872.* New York: Harper & Bros., 1873.

Janowitz, Morris. *The Community Press in an Urban Setting.* Glencoe, Ill.: The Free Press, 1952.

Karolevitz, Robert F. *Newspapering in the Old West.* Seattle, Wash.: Superior Publishing Co., 1965.

Knauss, James Owen. *Territorial Florida Journalism.* Deland: Florida State Historical Society, 1926.

Larsen, Arthur J. (ed.). *Crusader and Feminist: Letters of Jane Grey Swisshelm, 1858–1865.* St. Paul: Minnesota Historical Society, 1934.

The Lee Papers, A Saga of Midwestern Journalism. (By colleagues and associates as a tribute to E. P. Adler.) Kewanee, Ill.: Star-Courier Press, 1947.

Lindsay, Frank (Arthur L. Lane, ed.). *Observations From 46 Years of Newspaper Management.* Decatur, Ill.: Lindsay-Schaub Newspapers, Inc., 1960.

Lyford, Joseph P. *The Talk in Vandalia.* New York: Fund for the Republic, Inc., 1962.

Lynd, Robert S. and Helen M. *Middletown in Transition.* New York: Harcourt, Brace & Co., 1937.

Lyon, William H. *The Pioneer Editor in Missouri, 1808–1860.* Columbia: University of Missouri Press, 1965.

McLuhan, Marshall. *Understanding Media: The Extensions of Man.* (Signet Book, 2nd ed.) New York: The New American Library, Inc., 1966. Reprint of hardcover edition published by McGraw-Hill Book Co.

McMurtie, Douglas C. *The History of the Frontier-Index (The Press on Wheels).* Evanston, Ill. (mimeographed), 1943.

Meredith, Charles M., Jr. *The Country Weekly.* Boston: Bruce Humphries, Inc., 1937.

Moore, Clement, and Roe, Herman. *The First National Survey of the Weekly Newspaper Publishing Business in the U.S.* St. Paul: National Editorial Assn., 1929 (Reports also available for 1930 and 1932).

Moore, John W. *Moore's Historical, Biographical, and Miscellaneous Gatherings Relative to Printers, Printing, Publishing and Editing.* Concord, N.H.: Republican Press Assn., 1886.

Morgan, Arthur E. *The Community of the Future and the Future of the Community.* Yellow Springs, Ohio: Community Service, Inc., 1957.

————. *The Small Community, Foundation of Democratic Life.* New York: Harper & Bros., 1942.

Morland, Robert L. *Political Prairie Fire: The Nonpartisan League, 1915–22.* Minneapolis: University of Minnesota Press, 1955.

Nelson, Lowry. *The Minnesota Community: Country and Town in Transition.* Minneapolis: University of Minnesota Press, 1960.

Nelson, William. *Notes Toward a History of the American Newspaper.* New York: Charles F. Heartman, 1918.

Nichols, Ira A. *Forty Years of Rural Journalism in Iowa.* Fort Dodge: Messenger Press, 1938.

North, S. N. D. *History and Present Condition of the Newspaper and Periodical Press of the United States.* Washington: Government Printing Office, 1884.

Payne, George Henry. *History of Journalism in the United States.* New York: D. Appleton & Co., 1926.

Perrin, William Henry. *The Pioneer Press of Kentucky.* Louisville: John P. Morton & Co., printers for the Filson Club, 1888.

Polsby, Nelson W. *Community Power and Political Theory.* New Haven: Yale University Press, 1963.

Porte, R. T. *The New Publisher: A Tale of Twelve Cities.* Salt Lake City: Porte Publishing Co., 1924.

President's Commission on National Goals. *Goals for Americans.* (Spectrum Books) Englewood Cliffs: Prentice-Hall, Inc., 1960.

Radder, Norman J. *Newspapers in Community Service.* New York: McGraw-Hill Book Co., Inc., 1926.

————. *The Small-city Daily and the Country Weekly.* Bloomington: Indiana University Department of Journalism, 1927.

Rae, Walter. *Editing Small Newspapers.* New York: M. S. Mill Co. and William Morrow & Co., 1952.

Rand, Clayton. *Ink on My Hands.* New York: Carrick & Evans, 1940.

Ray, Grace Ernestine. *Early Oklahoma Newspapers: History and Description of Publications From Earliest Beginnings to 1889.*

University of Oklahoma Bulletin, New Series No. 407, Norman, 1928.

Rice, William B. (John W. Caughey, ed.). *The Los Angeles Star, 1851–1864*. Berkeley: University of California Press, 1947.

Ross, Murray G. *Case Histories in Community Organization*. New York: Harper & Bros., 1958.

Safley, James Clifford. *The Country Newspaper and Its Operation*. New York: D. Appleton & Co., 1930.

Scharf, J. Thomas. *The Chronicles of Baltimore*. Baltimore: Turnbull Bros., 1874.

Seeley, J. R., Sim, R. A., and Loosley, E. W. *A Study of the Culture of Suburban Life*. New York: John Wiley & Sons, 1956.

Smith, Bradford. *Why We Behave Like Americans*. New York: J. B. Lippincott Co., 1957.

Spayth, George W. *It Was Fun the Hard Way*. Dunellen, N.J.: The Spayth Press, 1964.

Spell, Lota M. *Pioneer Printer*. Austin: University of Texas Press, 1964.

Spring, Agnes Wright. *William Chapin Deming of Wyoming*. Glendale, Calif.: Arthur H. Clark Co., 1944.

Taft, William Howard. *Missouri Newspapers*. Columbia: University of Missouri Press, 1964.

Turnbull, George S. *An Oregon Crusader*. Portland: Binfords & Mort, 1955.

———. *History of Oregon Newspapers*. Portland: Binfords & Mort, 1939.

———. *Influence of Newspapers on the Economic, Social, Cultural and Political History of Pioneer Oregon*. Seattle: University of Washington Press, 1932.

Vidich, Arthur J., and Bensman, Joseph. *Small Town in Mass Society*. (Anchor Book) Garden City, N.J.: Doubleday & Co., 1960.

Watson, Elmo Scott. *History of Auxiliary Newspaper Service in the United States*. Champaign: Illini Publishing Co., 1923.

West, James. *Plainville, U.S.A.* New York: Columbia University Press, 1945.

Whetstone, Daniel W. *Frontier Editor*. New York: Hastings House Publishers, 1956.

White, William Allen. *The Autobiography of William Allen White*. New York: Macmillan Co., 1946.

Willey, Malcolm W. *The Country Newspaper*. Chapel Hill: University of North Carolina Press, 1926.

Williams, Walter, and Martin, Frank L. *The Practice of Journalism: A Treatise on Newspaper Making*. Columbia, Mo.: E. W. Stephens Publishing Co., 1911.

Williamson, H. L. *History of the Illinois Press Association*. Springfield, Ill.: Hartman-Jefferson Printing Co., 1934.

Winans, William H. *Reminiscences and Experiences in the Life of an Editor*. Newark, N.J. (no publisher given), 1875.

Winchester, Paul, and Webb, Frank D. (eds.). *Newspapers and Newspapermen of Maryland, Past and Present.* Baltimore: Frank L. Sibley & Co., 1905.

Young, John P. *Journalism in California.* San Francisco: Chronicle Publishing Co., 1915.

Young, Leilyn M. (Howard R. Long, ed.). *Fifty Years of Community Service: The Naeter Brothers and the Southeast Missourian.* Cape Girardeau, Mo.: Naeter Bros. Publishing Co., 1954.

Young, Samuel. *The History of My Life.* Pittsburgh: Herald Printing Co., 1890.

INDEX